C000132604

My
Culinary
Love
Story

Pauline Parry

First published in the United Kingdom and United States in 2022 by
Pauline Parry, in partnership with whitefox publishing

www.wearewhitefox.com

Copyright © Pauline Parry, 2022

ISBN 978-1-915036-28-5
Also available as an ebook
ISBN 978-1-915036-27-8

Pauline Parry asserts the moral right to be identified as the author of this work.

All rights reserved. No part of this publication may be reproduced, stored in a retrieval
system or transmitted in any form or by any means, electronic, mechanical, photo-
copying, recording or otherwise, without prior written permission of the author.

While every effort has been made to trace the owners of copyright material reproduced
herein, the author would like to apologise for any omissions and will be pleased to
incorporate missing acknowledgements in any future editions.

All photographs and illustrations in this book © Pauline Parry, unless otherwise stated.

Photograph on p. 5 by Megan Meza
Designed and typeset by Siulen Design
Cover design by Siulen Design
Illustrations by Janette Carpenter
Colour reproduction by Rhapsody Media
Project management by whitefox
Printed and bound by CPI Group (UK) Ltd, Croydon CR0 4YY

This book is dedicated to our grandsons George and Miles

They were my inspiration to write the journey of
why we left England to live in California

Contents

Prologue

My very first kitchen as a young single mother was above a bistro on a nondescript street in a small market town in England. To get to it, I had to go through the bistro's kitchen and climb a flight of stairs, making sure to duck my head to avoid bumping the beam at the top, which I did a little more often than I care to admit.

I never minded this less than glamourous entrance. Entering my new home this way constantly enveloped me in beautiful, comforting aromas – slow-roasted lamb, a delicate pie crust, the pungent whiff of freshly chopped garlic.

My little kitchen had a sturdy table, a few chairs and very simple cooking equipment. To me, it was heaven. It was here that I learned who I was and what I was truly made of. Up until then I had been someone's daughter, someone's wife, someone's mother. In this kitchen, at twenty-seven years old, I began to find out who I was as a woman and then as a cook. There would be other kitchens, other self-discoveries, but we never forget our first, do we?

In no time at all, I began to learn about the world of hospitality in England and later in America. My path wasn't a "career" as such. I never set out with a destination in mind. But I stayed sharp and took advantage of every opportunity that came my way.

There were many hurdles, which at times seemed insurmountable. And yet, I kept making it over each one. Soon I realized that all these obstacles only made me stronger and success in the culinary hospitality world came much like the hurdles – when I least expected it.

My love of food led me to Dennis, my husband now of more than forty years. And it led me to a job at a Michelin-starred restaurant in a castle that I helped convert into a hotel – an establishment that is still there and doing well today. It led me to the Napa Valley, where I learned more about wine from people such as Robert Mondavi. And it led me to a lifelong joy of burgers and margaritas on the beach in Malibu.

In this book, I share my story with you. Food is an important part of it, as is love. Both are the foundation on which my marriage and my business are built. It's the reason I say that everything I do has been guided by food, fun, and love.

I hope you will enjoy my story of where love and life can take you if you follow your passion and palate. As I said before, I didn't have a plan in the seventies except to explore my two loves – Dennis and hospitality, both of which brought me to America, where I'm writing these words.

There is no way I could have imagined any of this at twenty-seven, sitting at that little kitchen table above a restaurant while my children slept. I was so busy I didn't even have time to dream about the future. But then, dreams happen when you are asleep. In my culinary love story, I was always wide awake. The better to savor every delicious experience as it came my way.

CHAPTER ONE

An Unexpected Encounter

As the heavy wooden doors opened, the cold English wind and our first customers of the evening blew into Blostin's, a popular bistro in the quaint market town of Shepton Mallet, in the Mendip District of Somerset. I could hear Bill, the owner, chef, and my boss, suggesting I greet them out front. It was unlike me to ignore his instructions, but I shut it all out briefly, giving in to one more moment of delicious love with the lamb Bill had prepared for the night's menu. The best part of this job was that I not only got to see Bill at work in the kitchen, but, as we had a very small staff and I often did double duty as hostess and waitress, I also got to try all the food so I could answer questions about it when customers ordered.

I closed my eyes and slowly put another forkful in my mouth. It was his special braised lamb shank. Not only did it taste rich but the presentation was also beautiful. The lamb was served in a deep white bowl, embellished with a rosemary sauce made with a local dark beer and reduced for hours. The shank was placed on a helping of roughly mashed swede (which, when we had American customers, I made sure to call rutabaga), richened with butter, salt, and pepper. Roasted carrots finished with a rosemary sprig were served alongside. The aroma of the fresh rosemary begged me to breathe in this heavenly concoction as I took another mouthful.

I hadn't had many jobs in my twenty-seven years and this was my first at a restaurant. I had married at twenty-one, become a mother at twenty-three and again at twenty-four and divorced at twenty-six. Yet I had found myself instantly at home in the kitchen and the dining room – particularly on a day like today. It was the winter of 1977 and we were having a cold snap. The weather was perfect for the braised lamb special. The meat had been delivered that morning, prepared by the butcher with the bone in. I had watched as Bill tied string around the meat.

"This will keep the meat from falling off the bone while cooking," he explained as he deftly wound the string and tied it off in one easy move. "We need to keep the meat on the bone for presentation until the customer cuts into it and then it will fall off the bone." Ah yes, that moment of beauty that lets the customer know they are in the hands of a master.

"Chop chop, Pauline!" Bill's voice cut through my reverie.

"On it," I called back, reluctantly leaving the lamb to go and greet the customers.

He laughed as I made my way back into the restaurant. But there wasn't that much to do. It was about 6:30 p.m. and although it was winter and dark out since 4, the regulars never came in until about 8.

I found a couple waiting by the door to be seated. *A first date?* I wondered. This was the first time I had ever seen him or her. He had called earlier to be sure there was room and left his name – Dennis. He was quite tall and slender, with short blondish hair and a mustache. There was a twinkle in his blue eyes as he said hello and I found myself looking at him just a tad too long. He wore a brown corduroy jacket with leather elbow patches, a polo-necked sweater, gray slacks, and desert boots, which were in fashion.

He had his arm around the waist of the auburn-haired girl he had come in with. As they came toward me at the bar I thought, *damn, they look so happy. What a shame as he's quite dashing – my kind of chap.*

Like all guests, the couple had come into the bistro from the street through an oversize door fitted with a brass doorknob. The doors led not into the restaurant at first but to a small cozy cottage sitting room with a wood-burning fire, a large chalkboard menu and a small table with two chairs. There was a window seat, half draped with a red velvet curtain, and a chaise longue for guests to sit on. The bar had been converted from a pine chest, behind which we stored all the mixers. Behind the bar, a mirror alcove with shelving was filled with glasses and spirits.

I took the couple's coats and got them the drinks they ordered – Scotch for him, red wine for her – and then left them alone while they looked at the menu.

I fluffed the velvet drapes a bit as I walked back to the kitchen. The restaurant looked beautiful that night and the ambience was perfect for the French country food Bill served. The room was warm, romantic, and quaint, making it a perfect spot to take a date in Shepton Mallet.

I knew, because I had been on a first date here after my divorce. Andrew was the accountant of the building contractor I had taken a job with right after I split with my husband for good. He had a studious look and a shyness to him, which I think was why he could not always look me in the eye when we talked. But he did eventually get up the courage to ask me out and he took me to Blostin's. The owners, Bill and Monica, were also his clients and after dinner we joined them at the bar.

Bill and Monica were a hip-looking young couple. Monica was Greek, slender with big dark eyes and long curly black hair. She had a wonderful way of listening more than she talked and was always ready with a hearty laugh. Bill was tall and thin and never at a loss for small talk. He was very handsome, with a mustache and prematurely graying hair that made the ladies go gaga over him.

Although Andrew and I had no spark, Bill, Monica, and I did. The after-dinner drinks with them went on much longer than expected. At a certain point, the two restaurateurs disappeared for a while, leaving poor Andrew and I alone to try to make conversation again. I was understandably relieved when Bill and Monica returned, and just a little intrigued – they both had big smiles on their faces and were positively giddy. *Just what have they been doing*, I wondered. It soon became clear.

They had been talking about me, because as soon as they sat down again they both looked at me and together said, "Would you consider working here?" They looked at each other and laughed.

"Let's start again," Monica said, noting the look of surprise on my face. "We've really needed someone to help me with the management duties here. I just can't handle it all with the children getting older and needing more attention."

"Why me?" I asked, trying to stay calm but holding back my growing excitement. Andrew seemed completely nonplussed. "Well," Bill took over from Monica, "you clearly have a love of food, and you are so sociable. I've been in the restaurant business a long time and I can spot a natural – and you mentioned you are looking for something new."

I guess during drinks I had let more slip than I thought about my marital status. This was the seventies, I was in my twenties, and they were right – I was a newly divorced woman wanting something new in life.

My next question was, "What would I do?" Bill again took up the conversation. "Everything that Monica does. And we can give you the apartment upstairs to live in, as we've now moved out." I was speechless.

They went on to tell me all that she did and I listened in wonderment. They knew that I had been a secretary and that I had organizational skills. They liked my personality but that was all they knew. "Are you interviewing others?" I asked. Monica said, "We hadn't really thought about hiring anyone until we met you. We strongly feel you're the right one."

I told them I'd think about it and get back to them, but I knew almost immediately that I wanted this.

The drive back with Andrew was more or less silent as I thought of all that this might mean. I would have to uproot my children, Joanne and Ross. Would that be fair? After all, we had just settled into life without their dad. And I was fairly certain that my ex, David, would be livid at the thought of the children living above a restaurant. Not the most conventional of places to live.

What's more, could I cope with the two children and working all night? It would be some undertaking. I had never done anything like this before. It might not be right for me or the children, and yet... It seemed that what Bill and Monica had seen in me was something I felt was awakening in me – the ability to take on something new and thrive. Little did I know how ready I was to embrace this new feeling.

That night, after putting the children to bed, I called my mum and told her what had happened. She too was surprised but asked all the right questions. By the time I hung up, I knew it was what I needed to do. With the support of my parents, I felt ready to take this on. More than that, I was excited down to my toes for an adventure.

The next day, I met with Bill and Monica to talk over all the details and it was decided I would start in a month.

In a matter of weeks, I went from a house with my own garden and a community of neighbors and friends to living in an apartment above a restaurant. Unsurprisingly, David was angry at me for leaving a comfortable suburban home and choosing a noisy restaurant. Did I do it to spite him? No. I did it because I could feel the tug of adventure, the feeling I was meant for more than secretarial work, and a conviction that this would make Joanne and Ross interesting and happy children and, later, adults. I wanted them to see that one could take risks in life and still stand.

Speaking of standing, I was at that moment literally standing in my present and looking at my future. Although I had no way of knowing it at the time, I had just met the man who would become my husband and with whom I'd start a life together in America.

But right now, he needed to place an order with me for dinner for him and his date.

I whisked myself over to their table and put on my best smile.

"Have you decided, Den—?" I said. I caught myself before saying his name. Of course I knew it from his call earlier, but using it now would have been too presumptuous. *Take it down a notch, Pauline*, I thought to myself. The girl didn't notice but he did. Those eyes! His gaze made me blush a bit. Definitely flirting.

The auburn-haired girl was too caught up in the menu to notice, thankfully. She ordered the garlic bread straightaway. "I've heard it's wonderful," she said.

"It's a local favorite," I replied, nodding enthusiastically. "The chef starts with perfectly fat French baguettes that are cut down the center. The two halves are then bathed in melted local crystal salt butter that has been infused with fresh garlic." I had no idea why I was jabbering. All I know is that Dennis made me nervous. "Every bite then gets the perfect amount of butter and garlic."

They were watching me carefully, mesmerized by the description. Dennis even licked his lips. I couldn't stop myself, it seems. "Once the bread is soaked in the garlic butter, we pop it under the grill until the butter sizzles and the bread takes on a golden color. The final touch is a sprinkle of freshly chopped parsley. It's irresistible, you're going to love it."

"Maybe we should have two orders," he said with a laugh. "Although I might not be able to stand the smell of my breath in the morning." *He has a sense of humor*, I thought.

They ordered the lamb shank to go with the bread and the chocolate mousse topped with a layer of ganache for dessert and I nodded again. I was in full agreement with their order – it was delicious. I secretly hoped we wouldn't sell out of the lamb. I knew how good it was and was hoping to take some home to enjoy later with the children.

The children were one reason, or rather two reasons, that I was treading cautiously into any new romance. Getting into something serious was far from my mind but this Dennis fellow was making me rethink that.

That night I was both the greeter and the waitress, so after I took their order, I led the couple to the main dining room of Blostin's. It was just one step up and fitted with seven tables draped in brown velvet. The lights were dimmed and the warm feeling was heightened by the candles that glowed softly on each table.

Damn, I thought, *all this romance*. I was hoping their date wasn't more than that – I'd already started thinking I'd like to get to know Dennis more.

I gave them the best table in the restaurant, which was off to one side and by a window.

"My name is Pauline, if you need anything," I said, then flushed. It was such a simple sentence. How did I manage to make it sound like a come-on? I was always outgoing and positive but I had to stop myself. I didn't want to start something I wasn't able to finish. But it went by unnoticed, or so I thought. Dennis seemed more interested in the girl he was with. And yet, as I walked away, I saw him turn and watch me go.

Not that I felt there was anything too outrageous to look at. I was wearing a neat blazer and well-fitted skirt, with some patterned (possibly slightly saucy) hose. My hair was short – a layered bob with bangs – and I had on my signature Max Factor red lipstick. If pressed, I'd say I had some style. After all, I prided myself on being able to greet customers, take their orders, serve them dinner, and keep them happy in three-inch heels (never flats)! All the better to show off my slender ankles, which I have always felt are my best physical attribute.

When I brought the bread over, Dennis ordered another glass of Scotch. As the evening went on, he was without a doubt paying attention to me and it felt very good. I found myself flirting back a little too much. I was torn between feeling good about myself for the first time in a long time and feeling as though I was treading where I shouldn't.

As he was leaving, Dennis held my gaze as if he wanted to say something. To end the awkward silence, I said, "Well, good night. I hope you come back again soon." At the same time as I spoke, he said, "I'll be back again soon." We both laughed and then he turned to leave. Back then, cell phones were still a thing of the future so there were none of those "I'll text you" type of remarks. We had a landline in the restaurant, but I didn't even have a phone in my little apartment. I reasoned that if he wanted to see me again (which I was sure he did), he'd either have to call the restaurant or come by. Neither of those things happened.

Garlic Bread

Blostin's was known for this buttery French baguette infused with fresh garlic and garnished with chopped fresh parsley.

Serves 6

1 loaf (16 oz) French baguette
3 large garlic cloves, smashed
* and minced*

½ cup salted butter, melted

Cut the loaf in half horizontally and cut each half into three slices.

Stir the garlic into the melted butter. Dip each slice of bread in the melted butter and transfer to a baking sheet. Place under the broiler until sizzling and the crust is browned around the edges.

Transfer to a plate and sprinkle with chopped parsley.

Rosemary Lamb Shank with Rutabaga Mash and Roasted Carrots

This recipe is my adaptation of what I learned from Bill, the chef at Blostin's. As this was a French bistro in a very English village, of course its dishes were given a bit of a British slant.

Serves 6

Lamb Shanks

6 lamb shanks (each approximately
    ¾ pound)
2 tablespoons olive oil
1½ cups chopped yellow onions
1½ cups sliced carrots
10 garlic gloves, minced
1 bottle (750 ml) dry red wine
1 can (28-ounce) diced tomatoes
    with juices

2 cups chicken broth
2 cups beef broth
5 teaspoons chopped fresh rosemary
2 teaspoons chopped fresh thyme
2 teaspoons grated lemon zest
kosher salt and pepper

You will also need:
butcher's string

Wind string around each shank about three times and tie a knot to keep the meat secure to the bone. Sprinkle the shanks with salt and pepper.

Heat the oil in a large heavy pot over medium-high heat. Working in batches, add the shanks to the pot and cook until brown on all sides, about 8 minutes. Transfer the shanks to a bowl.

Add the onions, carrots, and garlic to the pot and sauté until golden, about 10 minutes. Stir in all the remaining ingredients.

Return the shanks to the pot, pressing down to submerge. Bring to a boil then reduce the heat to medium-low. Cover the pot and simmer until the meat is tender, about 2 hours.

Uncover the pot and simmer for a further 30 minutes, or until the meat is very tender. Transfer the shanks to a platter and remove the string.

Remove the vegetables with a slotted spoon and let the liquid reduce further for about 15 minutes, until thickened. Spoon over the shanks and serve on a bed of mashed rutabaga and roasted carrots.

Rutabaga Mash

2–3 pounds rutabaga, peeled and cut
  into 1-inch chunks
2 teaspoons salt

½ cup salted butter
½ teaspoon white pepper

Place the rutabaga chunks in a large saucepan and cover with room temperature water. Add one teaspoon of salt. Bring to a boil then reduce the heat, cover, and simmer for about 25–30 minutes, or until tender. Drain and let the rutabaga dry in a colander.

Mash the rutabaga with the butter, the remaining salt, and the white pepper.

Chocolate Mousse
with Chocolate Ganache

This dessert is just the right kind of sinfulness, perfect for a first date.

Serves 4

Chocolate Mousse

4 large egg yolks
¼ cup granulated sugar
2 cups heavy cream

7 ounces of semisweet chocolate chips
2 teaspoons vanilla extract

In a medium mixing bowl, using an electric mixer, whip together the egg yolks and granulated sugar on high speed until pale and fluffy, about 2 minutes.

Warm ¾ cup of the heavy cream in a 2-quart saucepan on the stove top over low heat (do not let it boil). While whisking the egg mixture, slowly pour in the warm cream to temper the egg yolks. Then return the combined egg yolk and cream mixture to the saucepan.

Cook over low heat, whisking constantly, for 3–5 minutes, until the mixture thickens just slightly and reaches 160°F. Remove from the heat and add the chocolate chips and vanilla extract. Stir well until the chocolate is melted.

Whip the remaining heavy cream until very stiff peaks form. Fold the whipped cream into the cooled chocolate mixture until well combined.

Place in four champagne coupes and chill.

Chocolate Ganache

⅓ cup heavy cream   *sea salt flakes*
⅔ cup semisweet chocolate chips

Place the cream and chocolate in a small saucepan and melt over low heat.

Once cooled, pour a thin layer over the chocolate mousse in the glass. Sprinkle with sea salt flakes and chill.

CHAPTER TWO

In the Mendips

While the children and I were happy in our new life at Blostin's, David and I continued to argue about how I had forced the sale of our home and relocated to Shepton Mallet. He didn't like it but there really was nothing left to say. What was done was done. My fears (and more importantly, his fears) for the children never came to fruition. They were more excited about living above a restaurant and sleeping in bunk beds than worried that they didn't have a traditional home.

As for me, on my first night on the job, when I got dressed in my cute dress and heels to report for duty, it seemed that the stairs from our apartment to the restaurant went on forever. Each step was another doubt in my mind. Yet by the time I got to the bottom, I was ready. It felt like I was going on stage. And there was Monica, waiting for her stand-in to see if I'd become a star. "I'm ready," I said to her with a smile. The fear disappeared immediately. Monica worked with me for a week then I was on my own.

And so it went. Each night after work I climbed the steep stairs to our apartment. This particular night I was happy that there were some of Bill's amazing lamb shanks left over. I brought home a bowl of them, which I put on the little kitchen table, and went to check on Joanne and Ross, who were fast asleep. I gave them each a kiss on their forehead. As usual, I had to bend down in just the right spot so I didn't hit my head where the ceiling slanted down.

I poured myself a glass of red wine and sat down to enjoy the lamb. My mind readily turned to the man I had met that night, Dennis. I smiled to myself. He had been flirting, hadn't he? I wondered if he'd call the restaurant or come by to ask me out. It had been so nice coming under the gaze of an adoring man, even if he turned out just to be a big flirt. Yes, I was hedging my bets a little. I didn't want to get my hopes up, but the feeling was sweet. It had been a long time since I'd felt like this and I loved it. I liked having a man in my life. It had been a year since David and I divorced. We had been married for five years. By all accounts, we were a happy couple, until we weren't.

David and I had met at a dance club in Bristol, where I had lived my entire eighteen years. He was five years older, slender, with dark brown hair, a cute smile, and a good sense of humor, and he was a carpenter by trade. Things moved fast – they always do at that age – and we married a little over three years later at a Catholic church in Westbury on Trym. I pored over the details for months. It was a big white wedding, with my sisters, Angela and Lesley, as my bridesmaids. I still remember the details – their dresses, the color of African violets, floppy hats and bouquets, which were a ball of flowers with white ribbon handles. My cousin Marcia, the flower girl, was in the same style dress but in white.

In our first year of marriage, David and I lived in an apartment at the top of a Victorian house in Redland, Bristol. It was quite gorgeous and although a small place it had a wonderful view overlooking the Downs. In that time, we saved enough money to buy a house in Radstock, where David's family lived. It was a neighborhood filled with first-time buyers, newlyweds, and people starting families. That fit us to a tee.

Two years after being married, I had Joanne at 23 and Ross at 24. The timing was fast, a surprise not only to me but to others. One day during my pregnancy with Ross, I was puttering in our garden when a neighbor I didn't know very well walked past. "Gosh, you haven't had the baby yet?" she asked. "Oh yes, I have a lovely daughter, Joanne. This is baby Number Two," I said as I patted my huge belly!

The neighborhood was perfect for a young mother. Everyone was starting families, which gave us a lot in common. We'd have coffee together in the morning, bringing our children over to one house or another. And we helped each other when we needed babysitting. We met and grew close to another couple, Sue and Mike, who also had two children. They were a lot of fun and we began having dinner parties.

The parties started as an excuse to get together, but I found that I absolutely loved to cook and create menus. I gained quite a reputation for making delicious food and I found myself pushing the envelope to come up with new dishes with new tastes and flavors for these gatherings.

It was during this time that I started to learn more about the importance of quality ingredients. We had a farmers' market once a week in the town and that was my first taste of fresh local fare. But my education as to the true bounty at my fingertips would come at Blostin's.

It was the seventies, and although women were beginning to find their own way in the world, I hadn't much noticed. I had been so busy with a husband at twenty-one and two children by twenty-four that I never had any thoughts whatsoever of what the future held for me. Having the children didn't give me much chance to think about it. As for work, I was brought up with the mentality that all a woman needed was secretarial skills. So, I got all my typing and shorthand certificates as well as bookkeeping and business qualifications, and left school at sixteen. After my divorce at twenty-six, I turned to these skills to make money – doing bookkeeping in the evening while the children slept.

Everything changed with my position at Blostin's. I loved everything about this new world of food and wine I found myself in and wanted to be the best, true to my father's advice that if you are to be a street sweeper, then be the best. This was far from sweeping the streets, but the sentiment was the same for me – I did all I could to learn everything and be the best. This often took me far and wide over the countryside in search of ingredients for that night's dinner.

In fact, I was heading out to the countryside the following morning to pick up some fresh cream and cheeses for the weekend menu. With only a few more hours to go before I would have to start a busy day, I went to bed to get some sleep, still thinking of Dennis and looking forward to perhaps seeing him at the restaurant the next day.

In the morning, I took Joanne and Ross to day care and set off for Wells. This cathedral city is nestled in the heart of the Mendip District of Somerset on the southern edge of the Mendip Hills, about twenty miles south of Bristol. The route from Shepton Mallet is one of those classically beautiful roads that England is so well known for, surrounded by green pastures parceled by hedges. There are massive oak trees here and there that give shade or shelter, depending on the weather, to those who walk through these fields.

The road, which is really a two-lane highway at best, is lined with hand-built gray stone walls that have been there for centuries. They have withstood time, runaway tractors, and the odd car accident. These walls are so solid that whatever ran into them came out of the skirmish crumpled and wrecked, while the stones took on barely a scratch.

Every so often the stretch of wall would stop for a driveway, or rather a dirt road, leading into a home or farm. That day, I drove down one of those roads to visit the dairy farmer, stopping in front of his rustic farmhouse. As many of these families did, the farmer lived in one part of the house while the back had been converted into a store with refrigeration. This was where they sold their products.

The entrance was a big wooden door, the top half of which was a glass window with six wooden dividers – perfect for peeking inside without necessarily going in. Conversely, they could see who was coming. The floor was paved with big square gray flagstones. I imagined them having to be scrubbed at the end of the day, à la Cinderella, with someone on their hands and knees with a brush and pail. On the wall behind a wooden counter were three long wooden shelves, each lined with Cheddar cheese wheels. On the counter there were large baskets filled with green apples. It was as if someone had asked for the most quintessential farmhouse design imaginable.

I loved walking in, being greeted by the sharp smell of Cheddar cheese and a friendly grin from the farmer. As usual, he was dressed in a long white cotton coat over his everyday wear of an open-neck checkered shirt and pullover, and brown heavy-duty trousers. He had his dark brown brimmed hat on, which just seemed to belong, and of course, his black wellingtons.

"Hello, Pauline. Lovely to see you and what a beautiful day it is today." Weather is always a big conversation starter anywhere in England. My stock reply was, "It's always great to see the sunshine break through for a moment, but it won't last."

"I have your usual order ready," he said, taking a long reach across the massive counter to look at the order pad. "Three gallons of heavy cream, plus six pounds of the salted butter, which I can divide up in one-pound increments for you." It was lovely of him to do this for me. It was not easy to divide the butter, which at this point was hard thanks to his professional refrigeration.

He brought the gallon buckets of cream to the counter and began dividing the huge slab of butter into one-pound pieces then wrapping it in white wax paper. I ordered a wheel of Cheddar as well, but then spied the apples. I took several pounds of those too, thinking an apple pie served with fresh whipped cream would be a perfect special for the night.

"Oh, I might just have to come by the restaurant and have dessert if that's the case, especially as apple season is at its peak," he said with a chuckle. He helped me load up the car and snuck in some apple cheese he wanted me to try. Feeling the full weight of happiness that comes with a car packed with culinary abundance, I waved him goodbye and headed home.

On my way back, I passed the local chicken farmer. I didn't have to stop there as he always came to us, delivering whole chickens in large wire baskets. They were free-range chickens so they lived a happy life fed on corn, which gave them a yellow color. Chef Bill and the sous chef, Adrian, would create their version of the French country recipes such as Coq au Vin, Herb-drenched Grilled Chicken, Chicken Casserole with Root Vegetables, Chicken in a French Onion Grainy Mustard Sauce, and so much more.

I knew many of these chicken dishes well. One in particular – Coq au Vin – had been one of my specialties for New Year's Eve when I was married. For birthdays we'd go out to a local restaurant or pub to celebrate, again with our neighborhood friends, but every New Year's David and I always had what we called a "fancy dress party." Everyone was invited and I would cook a feast for us all to savor.

In an irony not lost on me, as I was learning to cook and feed people's desires, I was losing my husband. And, yet another irony, it was at one of those New Year's Eve parties that I noticed David and Sue were hanging out together more than usual. Sue was plain with dark brown straight hair, cut in a bob with bangs. She had a quiet disposition and spoke softly, unlike me. She would always pause and think before she said anything.

So perhaps that was the attraction. I will never know for sure, but at one point during the evening, I went outside to throw away some of the empty bottles that were quickly accumulating – all of us loved to drink wine – and there they were, kissing.

My heart went to my throat and I had no idea what to say. I just turned around and went inside. As the Brits do, we went back inside to the party and carried on as if nothing had happened. When the party was over, I learned they had been seeing each other for six months. During a series of painful conversations, there was a moment I became so furious I threw a full bottle of milk at him. Luckily it missed him, but it was then that I realized I couldn't live like this anymore and told him to leave.

Thinking about it as I drove back from the dairy farm, the only thing I wished was that I hadn't wasted all that lovely milk on him, or rather on the wall.

When I finally told my mother what had happened, she was horrified and sad to think about what I had been going through. She wondered if my father might tell me, "You've made your bed and now you have to lie in it." Much to our surprise, my father was very understanding. As for David and Sue, it was on again, off again, as were David and I. It was all very strained, but I tried to keep it smooth for the children's sake.

After swearing to me the affair was over, he came home one night about midnight. I hate that this is all so cliché, but truly, I could smell her perfume on him. I confronted him, he denied it.

After going on like this for ten minutes, something just snapped in me and I could see clearer than ever.

"David," I said in a very calm, decisive tone, "this marriage is over. Tomorrow you will go to work as normal and come home. We'll have dinner with the children, put them to bed and then you will leave the house forever." And that is exactly what happened. I never shed another tear. He left and walked over the road to Sue's. Mike had already moved out.

It was at that moment I learned how strong I was. Life's lessons were coming at me fast, and I was excelling at handling them. But one of my culinary lessons came at a snail's pace, quite literally.

At Blostin's, I really was able to do everything there was to do in running a restaurant. Not only would I drive out along the Mendips for cream and cheese, but there were times when opportunities came to explore farther down that road, so to speak, for wilder fare. One of those times came early in the morning when I joined Adrian, Bill's sous chef, a burly heavyset chap with untidy ginger hair and freckles, on an adventure to look for the essential ingredient for that week's menu special – snails.

I am not a big fan of escargots but I will order them just for the garlic, shallot, and white wine butter to soak up with some great crusty bread. But I was intrigued to go on this adventure to see where and how one gets snails. Up until now, I had only had snails from a can.

Wrapped up in a rainproof mackintosh and my wellies, I journeyed with Adrian over the Mendips. We'd lift up the logs in the fields to find snails crawling over the damp, dark gray walls that lined the roads. We collected plenty, and put them in one of the white cream buckets that were left around from our visits to the farms. We always found a way to put them to use.

Adrian was enjoying my squeamishness a little too much. I put on a brave face as I reluctantly picked the snails off the wall. It was horrible. I felt the resistance as the snail's body clung on for dear life. I imagined it in anguish, hoping I'd just leave it alone. And then POP! The body would release and shrink back into the shell. The snail had given up the battle and even though I was wearing gloves, I tossed it into the bucket as fast as possible.

Adrian noticed my little tug of war with both my conscience and the snails. His laughter rang out clear in the quiet, dark morning. *Snips and snails and puppy dog tails*, I thought. The nursery rhyme suited Adrian perfectly at that moment. But far from embarrassing me, his merriment at my expense made me want to work harder to show him what I was made of. We stayed on task for an hour or two and between us we collected about 120 snails. Back at the restaurant, Bill had a system for ensuring they were edible. First he purged them for a few days, then rinsed them in plenty of water for another couple of days until he was satisfied that they were clean and ready to be prepared.

The process taught me that sometimes in the world of cooking, the things that taste delicious are not exactly a pretty sight to see and snails are one of them. As Bill finally began cooking them, I scrunched up my face and shook my head. *No way are those going in my mouth*, I thought. However, the experience only deterred me for a little while – I still order escargots, but mainly because they are the perfect delivery system for garlic and butter. And after all I had been through in my personal life with David, this was nothing. In fact, one more notch on my culinary belt made me happier, more independent, and ready for anything. Little did I know "anything" was waiting for me just around the corner!

Garlic Parsley Butter Escargots

The fruits of my labor in the Mendips were on the table that week at the bistro! Escargots shells covered with a garlicky white wine shallot parsley butter, served with a French baguette to soak up all the heavenly sauce.

Serves 8

1 cup salted butter

1 tablespoon dry white wine

1½ teaspoons kosher salt

½ teaspoon freshly ground
  black pepper

12 garlic cloves, very finely chopped

1 large shallot, finely chopped

¾ cup finely chopped parsley

24 extra-large escargots shells

24 extra-large canned escargots

Preheat the oven to 450°F.

Using an electric mixer on medium, beat the butter in a medium bowl until smooth (you can also beat by hand). With the motor off, add the wine, salt, and pepper, then beat on medium until incorporated. Reduce the speed to low, add the garlic, shallot, and parsley, and mix until just incorporated. Transfer the butter to a disposable pastry bag and snip off the end of the bag.

Place the shells in a single layer in a shallow baking dish and pipe about 2 teaspoons of butter mixture into each shell. Tuck a snail inside each shell then pipe in more butter mixture to fill the shell and mound over the top.

Bake the snails for 10–15 minutes, until sizzling. Serve immediately on a plate with crusty French baguette and a small fork to scoop out the snails. Enjoy dipping the bread in the extra garlic butter sauce!

Coq au Vin

This classic French dish is one of my favorites – braised chicken in red wine sauce with pancetta, garlic, carrots, mushrooms, and pearl onions. I served it often for neighbors at my annual New Year's Eve parties when I was married to David.

Serves 8

2 tablespoons extra virgin olive oil

4 ounces pancetta, diced

1 chicken (4-pound), cut into eight sections

1 cup sliced carrots (diagonal ½-inch slices)

1 cup chopped yellow onion

2 teaspoons salt

1 teaspoon black pepper

1 teaspoon chopped garlic

¼ cup brandy

½ bottle (375 ml) good red wine

1 cup chicken stock

10 fresh thyme sprigs, plus extra for serving

2 tablespoons room-temperature unsalted butter

1½ tablespoons all-purpose flour

1 cup pearl onions

1½ cups cremini mushrooms, stems removed, thickly sliced or halved

kosher salt and ground black pepper

Preheat the oven to 250°F.

Heat the olive oil in a large saucepan. Add the pancetta and cook over medium heat for 8–10 minutes, until golden brown. Using a slotted spoon, remove the pancetta to a plate.

Meanwhile, lay the chicken pieces on paper towels and pat dry. Liberally sprinkle the chicken on both sides with salt and pepper. Brown the chicken pieces in batches in a single layer for about 5 minutes in the same pan as the pancetta, turning to brown evenly. Remove the chicken to a plate with the bacon.

Add the carrots, onions, and the measured salt and pepper to the saucepan and cook for about 10 minutes, until the onions are lightly browned. Add the garlic and cook for a further minute. Add the brandy and return the pancetta, chicken, and any juices collected on the plate to the saucepan. Add the wine, chicken stock, and thyme sprigs and bring to a simmer. Cover the pot with a tight-fitting lid and continue cooking for 30–40 minutes on low heat until tender, then take off the heat.

Mash 1 tablespoon of the butter with the flour and stir into the stew. Add the pearl onions. In a medium sauté pan, add the remaining butter and cook the mushrooms over medium-low heat for 5–10 minutes, until browned. Add to the stew. Bring back to a simmer and cook for 10 more minutes. Season to taste. Serve hot with a sprig of fresh thyme.

Apple Pie

When apples are in season, it's difficult not to want to buy them all and bake every type of pie. The aroma of apples, cinnamon and pastry baking on a cold winter's day is intoxicating!

Serves 8

Dough

2½ cups all-purpose flour

4 teaspoons sugar

¼ teaspoon fine salt

14 tablespoons cold butter, diced

1 large egg, lightly beaten with 2 tablespoons cold water

Filling

3 pounds baking apples such as Granny Smith or Golden Delicious

2 tablespoons freshly squeezed lemon juice

⅔ cup granulated sugar

¼ cup unsalted butter

¼ teaspoon ground cinnamon

Generous pinch of nutmeg

2 tablespoons of crystal sugar (sprinkling pastry)

1 large egg, lightly beaten

In a medium bowl, whisk together the flour, sugar, and salt. Using your fingers, work the butter into the dry ingredients until it resembles yellow cornmeal mixed with bean-sized bits of butter. Add the egg and stir the dough together with a fork or by hand. If the dough is dry, sprinkle up to a tablespoon more of cold water over the mixture.

Form the dough into a disk, wrap in plastic and refrigerate until thoroughly chilled, at least one hour, or up to 24 hours.

To make the filling, peel, halve and core the apples. Cut each half into six wedges. Put in a large bowl and add the lemon juice and the granulated sugar, then toss to combine evenly.

In a large skillet, melt the butter over medium high heat. Add the apples and cook, stirring, until the sugar dissolves and the mixture begins to simmer, about 2 minutes. Cover, reduce heat to medium-low, and cook until the apples soften and release most of their juices, about 7 minutes.

Strain the apples in a colander over a medium bowl to catch all the juice. Shake the colander to get as much liquid as possible. Return the juices to the skillet and simmer over medium heat until thickened and lightly caramelized, about 10 minutes.

In a medium bowl, toss the apples with the reduced juice and spices. Set aside to cool completely.

Cut the dough in half. On a lightly floured surface, roll each half of the dough into a disc about 12 inches in diameter. Place a rack in the lower third of the oven and preheat the oven to 375° F.

Line the bottom of a 9-inch pan with one of the discs of dough, and trim it so it extends about 2 inches beyond the edge of the pan. Put the apple filling in the pan and mound it slightly in the center. Fold over the hanging pastry onto the apples. With the second disc of pastry, cut out apple shapes. Place over the pastry with a couple of apple shapes in the middle, directly over the apple mixture. Brush the dough with egg and sprinkle the crystal sugar over the pastry. Refrigerate for at least 15 minutes.

Bake the pie until crust is golden, about 50 minutes. Cool on a rack before serving.

CHAPTER THREE

A Snowy Christmas Eve

It was late afternoon on Christmas Eve. I was finished with the lunch service at Blostin's. Joanne and Ross were with their father and I was looking forward to an afternoon to myself.

My plan was to drive over to Cranmore, a neighboring village, where my friends John and Cynthia owned the Strode Arms, a popular pub housed in a building from the eighteenth century. There is a duck pond across the road from it that makes a picturesque sight as you pull up outside. Inside is an amazing inglenook fireplace so large it even has a stone side ledge that you can sit on. It was everything a pub should be.

While the law at the time dictated that pubs closed that day at 2 p.m., I took a chance that perhaps they were just clearing up from lunch and still there so I could give them a gift and say Merry Christmas.

I pulled up right outside the front door of the pub at 3 p.m. in my beautiful pearl-white MGB GT. The car was an extravagant splurge purchased with some of the money I made when David and I sold the house. True, with its sunroof, two seats, and back bench seat, it might seem a little impractical for English weather and a family of three, but, I told myself, this will be alright with the children for a couple of years. *Besides, life is for living*, I thought. I worked hard and a little bit of fun was good now and then.

As I opened the car door, the rich scent of a wood fire was in the air. I inhaled deeply. It was one of my favorite smells. Opening the doors to the pub, I heard the unmistakable sounds of a party. Chatter and laughter, glasses clinking and plates rattling. *So much for the law*, I thought, but it was the holidays, and the local pub is the perfect place to get in the festive mood. I entered and began to push through the bodies on my way to the bar and to find John and Cynthia.

From somewhere in the crowd, I heard someone say, "I know you. You're that girl from Blostin's." I turned around and there he was. Dennis.

He was even more handsome than I remembered from that night at Blostin's, and his eyes were bluer in the afternoon light. He was holding a gin and tonic and looking at me with a huge grin.

"I remember you," I said, trying not to appear too happy to see him, although I was. "You had dinner and left without coming back the next day."

He looked confused. "Had I forgotten something?"

"Yes! You forgot to ask me out!" I said, partly in jest.

There was no real response from him that I could figure out. Just a big grin on his face as he looked at me. I came to learn it was a smile fueled by gin, and a bit by seeing me. He'd been at the pub since that morning, celebrating the holidays over more than a few Bombay Sapphire gin and tonics. Oh yes, he was in a merry mood! After a few moments, I excused myself, saying I needed to find John and Cynthia.

I found them sitting at a table with other friends. John was one of those larger-than-life people. He had a strong presence whenever he walked in the room. Cynthia, on the other hand, was quieter. They both came from a sophisticated country background and were versed in the finer things in life. Their desire when they bought the property and the pub license was to elevate the culinary experience for their guests. They succeeded. Strode Arms now had a well-earned reputation for fine pub food using local ingredients, and was at the forefront of the gastro pub cuisine we know today.

As I approached them, they stood up and gave me a big hug. "Come and join us!" Immediately I had a glass of champagne in my hand. There were platters on the table filled with Stinking Bishop cheese, slices of venison sausage with apple mustard, a Double Gloucester cheese marbled with port wine, and a smoked trout mousse with tarragon, and I realized I was quite hungry.

Between bites, for some reason Dennis came into the conversation and I learned more about him. He was single and had had a flurry of girlfriends. He had his own carpentry business, and he was around thirty years old. He had been briefly engaged to a girl, but it hadn't worked out. So, I was right. It had been a date that night at Blostin's. I worried that he might be too much of a flirt but immediately put that thought out of my mind. I wasn't looking for anything serious so soon after my divorce. I was, however, looking for fun and would soon find out that Dennis was the perfect person for that.

As the afternoon wore on, the pub thinned out until it was just me, John and Cynthia, a few others, and Dennis. We all found ourselves sitting around the roaring fire, drinking champagne. John had opened a magnum of Lanson Black Label champagne and we all chatted and laughed. At one point, Dennis went outside. For a moment I wondered if he was leaving and tried not to give it much thought. I needn't have worried. He came back into the pub a moment later carrying a large armful of logs for the fire. He was covered with snow. Yes, snow! *Could this evening be more perfect,* I thought?

With snow falling, it was time to go. My little MG wasn't equipped to handle too much freshly fallen snow and, besides, I had to drive to Bristol, where I was picking up the children. As I started to gather my things, I felt Dennis come close to me. He needed a ride home, having drunk way too much that day. He lived around the corner from Blostin's on Cat's Ash Lane so it wasn't out of my way. I said yes immediately as I wanted to spend more time with him.

As we walked out to the car, he reacted as most people did, smiling at the impracticality of it in England and wondering how I'd come to choose it.

"I've always wanted one," I said, already anticipating his questions. "And it was so easy. I just called the local garage and ordered it. Actually, I ordered it in red."

Dennis just smiled. I could tell he was surprised and intrigued so I babbled on a bit, feeling flustered by his gaze.

"Well, I was ready to buy. The salesman asked if I wanted to come for a test drive. I said no, I knew what I wanted." Actually, and I didn't tell Dennis this at the time, when it came it was the most awful shade of red. I returned it and got the one I was driving that night – in pearl white. It was quite cute and just what I needed at this time in my life.

Again, he looked at me in such a way that I blushed. I hoped it was too dark in the car for him to notice. "I guess I'm a bit of a risk taker," I said with a hint of cheekiness. He pondered that for a moment and said approvingly, "Well, I do like this car."

By this time, snow was falling heavily. It was beautiful as it settled on the trees and turned the world a pristine white. I drove slowly on the slippery roads. We chatted about this and that and we were soon at his doorstep. As I put on the handbrake, Dennis leaned into me until our faces were almost touching. I leaned away.

"I have a confession," he said. *Uh-oh*, I thought, *what could that be about*? "I haven't stopped thinking of you since that night at Blostin's. It was that red lipstick."

I smiled, recalling my favorite shade of lipstick. "Can I have a Christmas kiss?" he asked.

I hesitated and, with just a hint of coyness, said, "No, my mother always told me not to kiss strangers."

"Ah, then let's not be strangers," he said. "Can I see you again? I'd like to take you out after Christmas."

"Yes, that would be lovely," I replied.

I drove on to Bristol to my parents' home that night. David had already dropped off Joanne and Ross. This would be the first time we would celebrate Christmas without him, but life was good, and I was in a place of joy and contentment.

My family home was a semi-detached bungalow that my father built in the late fifties. It was covered in light pinkish pebbles that were very popular at the time. As I arrived, I walked past my dad's garden, already glistening with the light snowfall and the white lights that he had put on the house to make it festive. Inside, I hung up my coat and went looking for everyone.

Coming home always felt good. My parents weren't well off, but they were hard-working and great providers for their four children. And they loved their home. In the lounge where we would all soon gather was a Christmas tree laden with multicolored lights, assorted ornaments, and silver tinsel. In the corner of the room was an upright piano. Funny thing, we all tinkered on this piano but none of us could play it.

My father grew vegetables in the garden that we would eat year-round. I was taught never to waste anything, so what we couldn't eat from my dad's increasingly large "harvest" in the spring and summer were preserved for fall and winter. As the oldest, I'd help the others string runner beans throughout the summer.

Those were frozen, while onions, eggs, and beetroot were pickled in malt vinegar with a little added sugar. They were then stored in large Mason jars that we got from the local newsagent store. I can't recall a time when we didn't have rows of tomatoes on top of the kitchen cabinets to ripen and turn into sauces or we would eat them like apples, adding a little bit of salt.

I found my dad in the kitchen. Beer in hand, he was tending to a roast turkey. He had already gone to the Polish butcher shop with the children – a family tradition he'd done with me and my sisters and brother for years – and bought sausages, cured meats, and blood sausage. We also always had a leg of meat of some sort, whether it was lamb or pork, as my mum and sister never ate poultry. On Boxing Day, there would be a stew called Bigos made with sauerkraut, bacon, kielbasa sausage, onion, and tomato. With Christmas day leftovers we'd make rissoles, a French dish that has been interpreted in British cuisine as a patty and, from our perspective, tasted like Christmas in a pie. And of course, we always had a Christmas cake, Christmas pudding, brandy butter, mince pies, and trifle.

In terms of how they liked to entertain, my mum and dad followed their heritages. My mother was English and my father was from Poland and had come to England after the war. He met my mother when he was twenty-seven and she was eighteen, the same age I was when I met my husband. Before I married, I was a Kaniecki.

My mother liked to entertain, but believed in serving exact quantities and always plated our food. It must have come from being one of sixteen children living on the poorest street in Bristol. But she was a very giving person and always made sure there was something on hand that was special to each person. That night, she had a cup of tea as she always did but had thoughtfully put out some wine for me.

My father was a bricklayer, and a fine one at that. He was a wonderful provider for us all. With his outgoing personality, he was the life of the party. While we couldn't afford to go out to eat, our house was always open to family and friends. As time went on, my father built quite a nice business for himself and we became more affluent. Rich or poor, though, my parents would always have an abundance of food in the house – pies, cold roast meats, casseroles, stews, cakes were always on hand for unannounced guests so they could offer hospitality to anyone who came across the threshold.

As I started to learn more about hospitality at Blostin's, I realized that I had a little bit of both my mum and my dad in me. I could see the wisdom in figuring out how much to make, like my mum does. For instance, Bill, a professional, swore by figuring out the right quantity for the evening's restaurant guests. But I also loved the casual style of my father's tradition of putting out a big roast and as much of the trimmings as the table could hold. He loved the table to look like a feast. And after all, who doesn't like leftovers?

I took a seat at the kitchen table with my mum and poured myself a glass of wine. "Where are the children?" I asked.

"In the lounge," Mum answered, sitting down next to me at the table. "They're feeling the Christmas presents, trying to work out what's inside the wrapping, and watching cartoons," she said. We chuckled and I called out to them that I was home. They ran up the passage toward me, giving me a big hug, and began to speak excitedly at the same time. They'd gone to the butcher's shop with Dziadek (granddad) to get sausages, and he had bought chocolate, nuts, and fruit for the holidays.

"You must be exhausted! And already in your pajamas, I see!" Mum had given them their baths and dressed them in their new red and white Christmas pajamas. Neither looked that excited about their matching outfits but I thought they looked adorable. "Let's go and watch the rest of the cartoon, then I'll read you a bedtime story and tuck you up for bed. We don't want to miss Santa Claus, do we?" They fell asleep before I could even finish the story.

When I got back, Mum was in the lounge with a cup of tea watching *Coronation Street*. Dad had gone around to the pub "for a quick pint", as he would always say. I got my wine and joined Mum.

"You look happy," she said. I know she expected me to perhaps be a little down about the holidays this year. "I'm glad," she said, a little to herself, but as a mother myself, I understood. She knew what I'd been through and was relieved that I had come out so well.

I told her about going to the pub, but not about Dennis. She smiled as she took a sip of tea and simply said, "And?" How did she do that? She could always tell when I had more to say. She asked how long I'd be staying.

"Actually, the restaurant is not opening back up until New Year's Eve, but I think I have a date before then." My excitement was showing through, despite my best try. "I saw this chap tonight who I had briefly met before and he asked me out. But the trouble is, he had a lot to drink and I'm not sure he'll remember he asked me out on a date."

But I'll be there in case he arrives, I thought to myself. And if he didn't turn up, I'd still have three whole days all to myself before the restaurant re-opened. I took another sip of wine, and a big breath in. I smiled as I let it go, relaxing into the holidays, my favorite time of year.

Smoked Trout Mousse

A perfect starter with flaky smoked trout lightly combined with chopped dill, aioli, finely chopped red onion, and celery, served with toast points.

Serves 2–4

8 ounces smoked trout, skinned, bones removed, and flaked
¼ cup finely chopped red onion
¼ cup finely chopped celery
½ cup aioli (garlic mayonnaise)

1 tablespoon freshly squeezed lemon juice
1 tablespoon finely chopped dill
kosher salt and white pepper
toast points, to serve

Mix the trout, onion, celery, aioli, lemon juice, and dill in a medium bowl. Season to taste with salt and pepper. Serve with toast points.

Pickled Beets, Onions, and Eggs

The pickling process for baby beets, shallots, and cage-free eggs can be a fun kitchen project. The results are very satisfying and beautiful. Enjoy these alone or accompanied by a cheese platter. They also are fabulous in salads.

Pickled Beets

1½ pounds small beets, including
  1 inch of the stem
1 cup malt vinegar
¼ cup sugar

¼ teaspoon kosher salt
½ teaspoon black pepper
6 sprigs of rosemary

Scrub the beets, place in a saucepan, and cover with room-temperature water. Bring to a boil, cover, reduce the heat, and simmer for 45 minutes or until tender. Drain and rinse with cold water. Trim off the stems, and rub off and discard the beet skins. Place the beets in a large bowl until ready to use.

Combine the vinegar and sugar in a small saucepan, bring to a boil, then cook over medium-low heat for 5 minutes or until the sugar is dissolved. Remove from the heat and stir in the salt, black pepper, and rosemary sprigs. Place the beets in a clean glass jar. Pour the vinegar mixture over the beets, let cool, then seal the jar tightly.

Pickled Eggs

12 eggs
1 cup malt vinegar
¼ cup sugar

2 teaspoons kosher salt
½ teaspoon black pepper
6 rosemary sprigs

Place the eggs in a large pot and cover with cold water. Bring to a boil and immediately remove from the heat. Cover and let the eggs stand in the hot water for 12 minutes. Remove from the hot water, let cool, and peel.

Place the eggs in a clean glass jar. Combine the vinegar and sugar in a small saucepan, bring to a boil, and cook over medium-low heat for 5 minutes or until the sugar is dissolved. Remove from the heat and stir in the salt, black pepper, and rosemary sprigs. Pour the vinegar mixture over the eggs, let cool, then seal the jar tightly.

Pickled Shallots

1 cup of malt vinegar   *18 small shallots*
¼ cup sugar   *½ teaspoon black pepper*
2 teaspoons kosher salt   *6 rosemary sprigs*

Place the vinegar, sugar, and salt in a saucepan, bring to a boil, and cook, stirring, over medium-low heat for 5 minutes to dissolve the sugar and salt. Add the shallots and rosemary sprigs and return the liquid to a boil. Remove the shallots and place in a clean glass jar. Pour the vinegar mixture over the shallots, let cool, then seal the jar tightly.

Hunter's Stew – Bigos

Not that he needed a reason, but my dad always used family celebrations as an excuse to make Bigos, a traditional Polish stew. Also known as Hunter's Stew, it combines kielbasa sausage and pork stew meat cooked with sauerkraut, tomatoes, carrots, spices, bacon, and green cabbage in a soul-satisfying dish.

Serves 6

4 ounces smoked bacon, chopped

1 pound kielbasa sausage, sliced into
   ½-inch pieces

1 pound cubed pork stew meat

flour, to dredge the pork

6 garlic cloves, minced

1 cup diced onions

1 cup diced carrots

2 cups shredded green cabbage

1 pound jar sauerkraut, rinsed
   and well drained

¼ cup red wine

1 tablespoon sweet paprika

1 pinch cayenne pepper

4 cups chicken broth

2 tablespoons tomato paste

1 cup canned diced tomatoes

sea salt and pepper

Place the bacon and kielbasa in a large saucepan over medium heat and cook, stirring, until the bacon has rendered its fat and the sausage is lightly browned. Using a slotted spoon, remove the bacon and sausage and transfer to a plate.

Dredge the cubes of pork lightly with the flour and fry them in the bacon drippings over medium-high heat until golden. Transfer to the plate with the bacon and sausage.

Add the garlic, onions, carrots, cabbage, and sauerkraut to the pan. Cook, stirring, for about 10 minutes, until the carrots are soft. Do not let the vegetables brown. Remove to a plate.

Deglaze the pan by pouring in the red wine and stirring to loosen all the bits that are stuck to the bottom. Add the paprika and cayenne and season with salt and pepper to taste. Cook for a minute. Add the chicken broth, tomato paste, and tomatoes. Heat through until just boiling. Return the bacon, sausage, and pork to the pan, cover, and simmer for about 2 hours, until the meat is very tender. Serve with the reserved vegetables.

CHAPTER FOUR

Our First Official Date

The holidays were lovely with my parents. Opening the presents on Christmas morning with the children and family was indeed magical. Even though this was the first Christmas without David, it was all quite perfect.

The night of our possible date came quickly and it was time to make tracks back to Shepton Mallet. I was still a little unsure that he would even remember asking me out, but I had said yes so I wanted to be ready if he did arrive. If he didn't show up, I was prepared to spend a quiet night by myself, enjoying the leftovers from the holidays and a glass of wine. I am quite content with my own company.

That morning I was up bright and early and got the children ready to be picked up. David would take them for the New Year. For the first time during the holidays, I felt a little emotional leaving them. I came to find out that it was harder on me than them. They seemed to be adjusting to the divorce well.

The departure was quick. A kiss and a hug, then their happy voices shouting "Bye, Mum!" out the windows as they drove off with David. Perhaps they were too young to realize what was going on, or perhaps they were truly OK with it. Either way, they were happy and so was I. Whatever had gone wrong in our marriage, David was always a good father.

My mum and dad helped me load up the car with my belongings, gifts, and enough leftovers to see me through to New Year's Eve. As I started the engine, I rolled down the window and laughed. "If I have my date tonight, I'll let you know how it goes." They smiled. "Yes, let us know," and with that I blew a kiss out the window and drove off.

I tuned the radio to my favorite classical music station, not wanting to be distracted by lyrics of Christmas carols or love songs. I felt relaxed and in a good mood. Was I excited about going on a date? I believe I was, and I might feel disappointed if he did not turn up.

I had no work duties until New Year's Eve, which felt quite delightful. Of course, living above the restaurant meant I could never really leave work behind, but I had made an effort to ensure everything was in place for New Year's Eve so I could have time to enjoy the intervening days with no responsibilities.

I arrived home much quicker than I expected. I'm sure I had been daydreaming the entire trip. All the beautiful snow that had fallen over the holidays was now turning slushy and dirty, and it was cold. I shivered as I retrieved everything from the car. I pushed open the door and turned on the lights. In the cold light of day, the restaurant was much less romantic. I took a quick glance around to see if everything looked OK, and it was all just as I had left it on Christmas Eve. Even the menu was already written on the chalkboard, ready for New Year's Eve.

It was getting dark as I made my way upstairs to the apartment. I closed the drapes and turned on the gas fire to make the place cozy and warm. I threw my coat over the sofa and put on the television, just to have some sound in the background. I unpacked and put everything away in its rightful place as I wanted to make sure all was neat and tidy should I decide to invite Dennis up for a nightcap at the end of the evening. *I need to be prepared*, I thought.

I got myself comfortable, putting on my candlewick robe and sheepskin-lined slippers. It was a practical look that did the job of keeping me perfectly warm. I put the kettle on and made myself a cup of tea, then realized I was quite hungry. Maybe I should heat some of the leftover lobster soup? Yes, that would be perfect. With my cup of tea and bowl of soup in hand, I contemplated my plan of action for the next few hours.

First up – what to wear. I found a long-sleeve beige and black shift-style dress with a turtleneck band. This could work nicely. The dress had a peephole cut out at the back, and a zip.

I put out my new black underwear, black patterned hose, and, to finish the look, my black knee-high boots. I laid everything out on the bed, making sure the combination looked right. Yes, this would do nicely. Then I got ready for a bath and some pampering.

By 7:30 I was fully dressed. I took a final look at myself in the full-length mirror and thought, *This is as good as it gets, Pauline. I think it will do, I hope Dennis thinks so also.* I poured myself a glass of Muscadet and watched television distractedly, waiting for the doorbell to ring.

It rang at 8 p.m. on the dot.

I ran down the stairs, pulled open the door, and there he was – "Well, hello!" I found myself looking at him longer than needed and wondering, had he gotten taller? His smile was big, his blue eyes just as mesmerizing, and his cleft chin even more pronounced. I loved the casual way he had turned up the collar of his sheepskin coat and that his hands were in his pockets. And then I said, "I wasn't sure you'd show up." His eyes got a little bigger and his smile even wider. "I probably deserve that comment. I was pretty toasted the last time I saw you."

"Give me a minute, I'm almost ready," I said, leaving him in the restaurant's sitting room while I ran upstairs to get my things. I returned with a coat and gloves on. "Let's go!" I followed him out the door and locked it behind me.

He opened the passenger door of his car for me, then closed it. As he got in himself, he said, "I thought we would go to the Crossways Inn, have you been there?" I hadn't been there, but Bill and Monica had mentioned it several times.

The inn was built in the seventeenth century and is in the middle of nowhere. To get to it, we had to drive through a maze of one-lane roads with tall hedges. It was a bit scary, especially in the dark. If anything came the other way, I wasn't sure how we would pass each other, but fortunately that didn't happen. We eventually came to the end of these narrow roads and, as we approached the inn, found ourselves in a large open space with just the inn and a generous parking lot. Up until the late nineteenth century, in the era of fairs and animal markets, it had been a calling stage for coaches and carriages. Now, it was a charming cottage that had been converted into an inn with dark wood beams and an open fire, which was roaring when we came in. Like Blostin's, it was old, and it wore its age more as a sign of beauty than neglect.

The restaurant was full but there was an opening at an inviting little settee that looked comfortable, with several cushions thrown on it and a low coffee table in front of it. We agreed it was the perfect place to sit. As with all inns, orders were taken at the bar. I asked Dennis to order me a red wine, Rioja if they had it. He laughed. "I love a woman who knows exactly what she wants," he said.

Once settled, we both held up our glasses, looking into each other's eyes for a moment. "Cheers," we said together, taking sips and getting comfortable. As we did, we moved closer together.

Our evening was filled with conversation and wine, and both flowed easily. "Oh my," I said suddenly. "We should probably eat something – the kitchen will close soon." We were so wrapped up in our conversation and each other that we hadn't even thought of eating, but food was a good idea. I always loved to try new things from local inns, either for ideas or simply just to know what they offered, and I usually ordered more than we could eat just to see the presentation and have lots of tastes.

We ordered Chicken Liver Pâté with Port Wine Gelée. It was served in a small canning jar with a glass top that hinged open. I spread some on the crostini that came with it and could instantly tell that they had made it with a copious amount of butter. It melted on my tongue and the port wine jelly added the right amount of sweet. Heaven. There was also Cheddar cheese from a local farmhouse served with a cute cottage loaf that was still warm. We broke it open with our hands and made perfect bites with the cheese, pâté, salted butter and house-pickled onions, which were served in a small ramekin.

With all the food, wine, and talk, I was beginning to feel things were going well, very well. *Still*, I wondered. I had not really dated since the divorce and now here I was, a divorcee with two small children. As much as I didn't want to pour out my whole life story on a first date, parts of it were unavoidable. But my marriage with David felt like a lifetime ago, and I was so happy living above the restaurant with Joanne and Ross, who needed to go back there? I really felt I was on the verge of a new life and loved being out and dating again.

We shared our stories, laughed, drank, and ate. We were gently getting to know each other, and I was feeling so comfortable, that before I knew it I just blurted it out. "Oh, by the way, I have two children. Joanne and Ross."

I thought he was going to take a bite out of his beer glass. He didn't, but the shock on his face was indeed a picture. "Oh, really?" he said. "Really," I answered. "They are three and four and are quite fabulous. True, it can be quite hard at times balancing work, children, and play, but I'm getting used to it." I rushed to get all the details about them in one breath.

There was a bit of a pause, with neither of us saying anything. It was like Dennis was processing what I had just said. I changed the subject and asked him what his plans were for the rest of the holidays, all the while wondering if he was asking himself what he'd gotten into. He probably wouldn't want to get involved.

We moved past my announcement without really addressing it much more and then we noticed we were the last people in the bar. "We should probably go," I said. We said good night to the land-lord, and Dennis held my hand as we braced ourselves to walk out into the cold night air and back onto the road.

As we pulled up outside of Blostin's, my mind was working overtime, wondering if I should ask him in or not. But for the second time that night, I surprised myself by blurting out, "Would you like to come in and have a cup of coffee or a glass of port?"

Of course he did and, as I poured us a glass each of Taylor's L.B.V.R. port, I thought about music. I put on my favorite tape of the moment, *Nilsson Schmilsson*. I loved the song "Without You," which was all over the radio. *I hope he doesn't think I'm being forward by putting on romantic music. But why should he? This is perfect music for this time of day, or rather, night. Besides, I like it. Oh my, I am feeling a little nervous.*

I had no need to feel that way. We picked up where we left off at the pub without a beat. I was drawn in by his presence and fasci-nated by his perspective of whatever he talked about.

As I reached over to refresh our port, he caught me halfway to his glass and gently kissed me. With his hand still on my cheek, we looked at one another for a moment as if to say, did that really happen? It did, and I felt my body pull closer to his as he brought me in tighter for another kiss. And another. Oh my, I was sinking in, but then, just like that, I pulled back. "Maybe we should call it a night." I wasn't quite as ready for this as I thought I was.

Reluctantly, he pulled away. "You're probably right, but I really don't want to leave, you must know that." I smiled, knowing exactly what he meant. I really didn't want him to leave either.

It was clear we could end up kissing all night long, and this was much too early in the relationship – if it even was a relationship. I still wasn't sure what he thought about dating someone with children, and I definitely did not want him to be a one-night stand. I was attracted to him and wanted to see him again.

We walked down the stairs into the sitting room. He pulled me into him and gently kissed me on the forehead. "When can we meet again?" he asked.

My mind was racing to give him an answer, thrilled at the prospect of seeing him again. I calmly replied, "How about New Year's Day? Start the year together?" Was that too much?

Happily, he smiled and said, "Great. I was planning to go to the Carpenters Arms in Pensford – maybe a Bloody Mary might be in order after New Year's Eve, and we can have a spot of lunch there also?"

"It's a date," I said, smiling.

He got his coat on, ready for the cold night air. At the door, he turned toward me once more, kissed me, and then slowly moved away. As I watched him walk down the street, he pulled his collar up again, put his hands in his pockets, and picked up his walking pace.

Once he turned the corner, I stepped back into the restaurant, locked the door, leaned against it, and said out loud, "Pauline, that was indeed a fabulous evening!" With that, I ran upstairs and got undressed, throwing my clothes on the floor. I snuggled under the bed sheets, completely naked except for the big smile on my face, and drifted happily into a deep sleep.

Lobster Soup

First dates call for a little decadence, such as this creamy lobster soup served with fresh poached chunks of lobster.

Serves 4

4 cups poached lobster tails with shells
 for the stock (you can usually get
 precooked lobster from any good
 fish monger)
6 cups of water
½ cup each chopped celery, carrots,
 onions
6 tablespoons unsalted butter
6 tablespoons all-purpose flour

½ cup finely chopped celery
4½ cups whole milk
1½ cups lobster stock from cooking
 lobster
1½ cups chopped brown onion
1 tablespoon chopped chives,
 for garnish
sea salt and white pepper

If the lobster is not precooked, place the water in a large saucepan with the celery, carrots, and onions. Bring to a boil and add the lobster tails. Poach at a simmer for 10 minutes. Remove the lobster from the water. Remove the shells and return them to the water to create the stock. Continue cooking until reduced to 2 cups.

Chop the lobster and strain the stock of shell and vegetables.

Melt the butter in a saucepan. Stir in the flour, finely chopped celery, and salt and pepper to taste. Blend well. Very slowly mix in the milk and lobster stock. Add 3 cups of chopped lobster and the chopped brown onion. Cook for 10 minutes over medium heat.

Divide the remaining cup of lobster meat between four bowls, pour lobster soup into each bowl, and garnish with a pinch of chopped chives.

Chicken Liver Pâté with Port Wine Gelée

This is very close to the creamy chicken liver pâté Dennis and I shared on our first date. I love it topped with a port wine gelée served with crostini.

Serves 6

Chicken Liver Pâté

9 tablespoons unsalted butter, softened
1 large yellow onion, finely chopped
1 pound chicken livers, trimmed
  and halved
2 teaspoons kosher salt
½ teaspoon freshly ground
  black pepper

1½ tablespoons minced fresh thyme
1 cup tawny port
1 teaspoon lemon juice
kosher salt and pepper (optional)

You will also need:
plastic wrap

Heat 3 tablespoons of the butter in a large skillet over medium heat. Add the onion and cook for about 5 minutes, until softened. Transfer to a food processor.

Increase the heat to medium-high and add 3 more tablespoons of the butter to the skillet. Add the chicken livers and cook for about 2 minutes, until the exteriors are no longer pink. Add the salt, pepper, and thyme. Cook for a further minute, or until the livers are lightly browned and firm but still slightly pink inside. Add the contents of the skillet to the food processor.

Pour the port wine into the skillet and bring to a boil over high heat. Reduce to about 2 tablespoons. Add to the food processor and process until smooth. Press the mixture through a fine mesh sieve, cool to room temperature, and whisk in the remaining 3 tablespoons of butter and the lemon juice. Adjust the seasoning if needed.

Transfer to a serving dish, cover with plastic wrap, and refrigerate for at least 3 hours.

Port Gelée

½ teaspoon granulated gelatin   *1 cup port wine*
¼ cup cold water

Sprinkle the gelatin over the water and allow it to bloom (fully hydrate), about 10 minutes. Over low heat, bring the port wine to just a simmer, then remove from the heat. Mix the bloomed gelatin into the warm port and let cool to room temperature.

Pour the cool port gelée over the chilled liver pâté and return to the refrigerator until set, about 3 hours.

Bloody Mary

The perfect hair of the dog on New Year's Day! Tomato juice shaken over ice with spices and hot sauce with a squeeze of citrus, served in a tall glass rimmed with celery salt.

Serves 1

celery salt to rim the glass
2 lemon wedges
1 lime wedge
2 ounces vodka
4 ounces tomato juice

1 teaspoon prepared horseradish
2 dashes Tabasco sauce
2 dashes Worcestershire sauce
freshly ground black pepper
ice, for shaking

Garnish

2 green olives, speared on a toothpick
lime wedge
celery stalk

Pour celery salt onto a small plate. Rub the juicy side of one lemon wedge along the rim of a tall 12-ounce glass. Roll the outer edge of the rim in the celery salt until fully coated then fill the glass with ice and set aside.

Squeeze the remaining lemon wedge and the lime wedge into a shaker and drop them in. Add the vodka, tomato juice, horseradish, Tabasco, Worcestershire sauce, and a pinch of freshly ground black pepper, along with some ice cubes, and shake gently.

Strain into the prepared glass. Garnish with the speared green olives, lime wedge, and celery stalk.

CHAPTER FIVE
Children and Dating

Once I became a working single mother, I mastered the art of multitasking. Even when I was married to David, it had been a surprise how fast things changed when the children came into our lives. The freedom of doing what you liked when you liked no longer existed.

And yet, when you are in the thick of it all, you just get on with it. Everyone likes to focus on hardship, but there was a lot of joy, that's for sure. I was independent, I was supported by my family, I had two beautiful children who liked our new lifestyle and who loved and took care of each other.

For the first time in my life, I was in charge. I had no one to answer to but myself. Of course, the children were the most precious part of my life and the center of it all, even with work and a few dates. And honestly, I loved the attention I was getting from men. I was in full bloom as a young lady and I liked the way I looked and dressed. I think I was attractive. Not beautiful, but attractive. I hadn't felt attractive to my husband and certainly his affair made me doubt myself as a woman.

Was my attitude remarkable? When I look back now, yes. The seventies were such an interesting time for women. We questioned whether we could have it all, which of course is not easy. But I never gave that a thought as I was drenched in the ocean of life. Sometimes the sea turned a little rough, but my life was going in a direction that was different to that followed by most of the people I knew. Old friends and ways of being were falling away, and in their place a new life was emerging, and a new me.

After being separated from David for seven months, and living above the restaurant for four months, the children and I fell into a solid routine. The struggle of changing homes and finding a nursery school, and the emotion from the upheaval faded into memory, and we found our own rhythm.

Most mornings they'd get out of their beds around 7:30 and join me in mine. After a little rough and tumble, it was time for breakfast and getting dressed. Joanne was now good at doing this herself, but I still helped Ross with a few details. Then I'd throw on a pair of jeans and a top and, depending on the weather, we'd put on our coats and hats and we were out the door and down the street, me holding each of their hands on either side of me.

The daycare school was only a few hundred yards away, in a converted Victorian house. The children seemed happy there. Being so close in age, they got on together well and were a tremendous support to each other.

Once they were settled in, I'd return to the restaurant to tackle the tasks of the day, then pick them up around three. We'd spend time together and after dinner I'd bathe them and read them a nighttime story. All of this had to be done by 6 p.m. so I could be ready for work when the restaurant opened. Sometimes I would tuck them up in bed before going downstairs, and other times I would let them play and come up later to tuck them in. Throughout the night, I would run upstairs to check they were OK and sleeping soundly. And if they ever needed me, all they had to do was wander downstairs.

This went on Monday through Friday, except for Tuesday, when I had the night off so could stay upstairs with them. If I decided to go out on a Tuesday, I would bring in a babysitter. I found a high-school girl called Patricia, who was within walking distance of us. The children got on well with her, so that seemed a perfect solution for me to have some free time if I so wished.

On the weekends, David would pick them up Saturday morning and then bring them back Sunday about 6 p.m. I worked Saturday to prepare for the evening service and, of course, worked the evening, finishing usually about midnight. Sunday was my day off, but I had to be back in time to meet the children when David brought them home. My life truly revolved around the children and work, with limited time for dating, meeting friends, and shopping.

I had no problem with this situation as I had found a new lease of life and was completely absorbed with this new career that had fallen in my lap. I quickly realized this was my future. While yes, it was technically "work", it never felt that way to me. I loved every minute. I tried to learn everything I could about managing a restaurant, safety and sanitation, cooking techniques, and people. I couldn't get enough. When the chefs called in sick, I stepped in to make desserts and help to prep the main meals in the kitchen. If the waitress couldn't make it in, I doubled up on my tasks – taking orders, serving, and wishing guests good night.

Once I got used to the routine and was more acquainted with the job, I did find some time for dating. I had a few admirers and went out on several dates. I was curious as to what single life was all about and, at the time, didn't want to limit myself to one man. *The more the merrier*, I thought.

But Dennis was always there between dates. I began to feel I wanted to spend more time with him than any of the other men who were swooping in and out of my life. In fact, I was finding dating tiresome, as most of the men I met were dull compared to Dennis.

Almost without realizing, I was slowly building a romantic relationship with Dennis. Over the next ten months we regularly went out to restaurants and he matched my love of food and wine. We found mutual joy in dining out and it was a fabulous time for us.

Before I knew it, we'd been seeing each other for two years. To celebrate our second anniversary and my thirtieth birthday, we had an amazing over-the-top dining trip to London. We traveled there on a commuter train, dressed up in all our finery amid all the businessmen in their bowler hats reading newspapers while we indulged in pink champagne. We stood out like sore thumbs, but we didn't care. It was my birthday, a time for celebration.

At one moment in the weekend we walked around Trafalgar Square being silly, a little bit giddy with laughter. I was feeding him a red apple. Between bites, he suddenly picked me up and swung me around and around in his arms. As he put me down, he said, "When you're forty I'm going to hire the Concorde and take you to New York! We'll stay at the Plaza and we'll eat at the Waldorf Astoria!" He shouted this out for all to hear. We giggled together at the thought of such an adventure. "Let's put it in the calendar!" we told one another, laughing. We continued walking and I put my arm in his, content. Silently, I mused: *Forty seems so very far away right now.*

It didn't hurt that seeing Dennis had a little bit of convenience built in – he lived just around the corner from the restaurant, which made it easy for him to join me there after service. Bill would be there, and sometimes Adrian and Monica also. We'd hang out together for an hour or two or more, depending on what night of the week it was. Dennis being there was part and parcel of our dating. If he wasn't there, someone would ask, "Where's Dennis?" He was beginning to feel like a boyfriend, but in quiet times I'd ask myself if I wanted him around forever. It felt much too soon for someone else to come into my life permanently.

That said, the first time I invited him to the apartment for dinner, I had the feeling of a serious turn in our relationship. It was my night off, a Tuesday evening. I was dressed in jeans and a sweater and was walking about barefoot. Normally the children would be home, but on this night they had a sleepover at a friend's house. As I put out nibbles in the lounge and set the dining table in the kitchen, I could hear the noise of the restaurant below – a mixture of laughter and talk. The aroma from Bill's dinner that night was making its way up the stairs, teasing me with the scent of herbs, garlic, and chargrilling, making my taste buds come alive. *Maybe I should have ordered food from the restaurant?* I thought for a moment. Too late now. Would Dennis love my dinner? *Well, he either will or he won't*, I muttered quietly to myself.

Before I had much more time to think, Dennis came in through the back door of the restaurant. I heard him say hello to Bill and Adrian as he passed by the kitchen. I was at the top of the steep stairs, ready to greet him as he ran up. He handed me a bottle of wine. "It's a very special Saint-Emilion," he said. "I've been waiting for the right time and the right person to share it with."

No sooner had I placed the wine on the coffee table and turned toward him than he took my face in his hands and kissed me. I closed my eyes and then opened them as he let his hands drop by his side. Oh my. This was a good beginning to our dinner. I smiled and found the corkscrew. "Maybe we should open this now to let it breathe," I said, fully aware that we might also need a moment to breathe. "This will be perfect with dinner."

Dennis took control of opening the wine, making sure he didn't shake it and disturb any sediment. While he was doing that, I asked, "Would you like a gin and tonic? I think Bombay Sapphire is your favorite, right?"

"You remembered! That would be great," he said.

This was the first time I'd ever made a drink for him. I went into the kitchen to prepare the gin in a tall glass with a slice of lemon and Schweppes tonic water. I already had a bottle of Chablis chilling in the bucket in the living room.

It seemed we always had so much to talk about, whether it was the wine, how our day was, the children, anything. He was very easy to talk to and had a wicked sense of humor that always made me laugh. Then out of nowhere I suddenly glanced at my watch and took a deep breath. "I've lost track of the time! It's already eleven. You must be starving," I said.

"Famished!"

I was already walking toward the kitchen, where I'd prepared a salad of arugula with bibb lettuce, avocado, finely chopped mint, and crumbs of Stilton, all ready to toss with a Dijon vinaigrette I'd made myself. In the oven I had Dauphinoise Potatoes slowly cooking. Instantly, I was glad I'd chosen that style of preparation for the potatoes. This dish can withstand a little overcooking. All I needed to do was pan-char two beef tenderloin steaks and finish them with an au poivre sauce.

I put the potatoes on the table, placed our two dinner plates in the oven to warm, and tossed the salad as the steak was cooking. When it was ready, I poured brandy over the steak and set it on fire. Always a showstopper, and it caught Dennis's attention from where he sat in the lounge. I was busy, but I heard the "wow" from him. When the flame subsided, I added heavy cream and pepper-corns with a squeeze of lemon and then let the sauce reduce to the right consistency and a rich brown color. I put the steak on the warm plates with a liberal helping of peppercorn sauce and sprin-kled some chopped parsley on top. I put my head around the door to the living room. "Ready! Bring the wine."

By the light of a few votive candles, dinner looked positively glor-ious. "How did you muster this all up in ten minutes? It's a feast!"

"I'm a professional, remember?" I said with a smile.

And he kissed me again.

"Let me pour the wine," he said. He poured a little into his glass first, to taste and make sure it was good. "I think you'll like this – it tastes perfect, full bodied with black cherry fruits," he said, pouring wine into my glass. As he poured, the wine made my favorite sound. "That 'glug, glug' with the first pour from a bottle always makes me smile," I said. He topped up his own glass and with a "Cheers!", we started dinner.

You know that adage, you win a man's heart through his stomach? I'm pretty sure that was the night I won Dennis's heart. He devoured every little bit of his dinner. I impressed him and I wondered if any of his other dates had done that for him. He must have heard my thoughts. "Peeps," – he'd started calling me this a little while back – "that was really lovely. I've never had anyone do that for me before." He kissed me again and together we savored the last drops of the beautiful wine. Dessert was a choux puff filled with whipped cream, topped with chocolate ganache. "Can this get any better?" he asked, laughing.

During the whole time we had been dating, Dennis still had not met Joanne and Ross. Why complicate things by bringing the children into the scenario? I was still not ready for another commitment, even though our relationship had been getting better and better. That night, I guess he'd been thinking the same thing. He asked me the question I'd been avoiding. "Peeps, I'd love to meet Joanne and Ross. I feel as if I know them. What do you think?"

I answered without hesitation, "Not just yet. I think we need a little more time. I'll let you know when the time is right."

He was disappointed, but I was in no hurry to bring Joanne and Ross into the mix of this love affair. With that, I gave him a kiss to distract him from continuing this conversation.

Steak au Poivre

There is nothing better than Steak au Poivre for going right to a man's heart! A seared beef tenderloin steak with a green peppercorn and cognac cream sauce, served with Dauphinoise Potatoes and accompanied by a mixed green salad with Dijon vinaigrette, is the perfect Cupid's arrow.

Serves 4

4 tenderloin steaks (8-ounce),
  1 inch thick
2 tablespoons coarsely cracked
  black peppercorns
kosher salt
1 tablespoon unsalted butter
1 tablespoon extra virgin olive oil

⅓ cup cognac, plus one teaspoon
1 cup heavy cream
1 tablespoon green peppercorns in brine
salt

You will also need:
aluminum foil

Remove the steaks from the refrigerator 30 minutes prior to cooking. Spread the crushed black peppercorns on a plate. Salt the steak on both sides. Press both sides of each steak into the crushed black peppercorns, to coat.

Melt the butter and olive oil in a large skillet over medium heat. Add the steaks. For a medium rare, cook for 4 minutes on each side. Once done, remove the steaks to a plate, tent with foil, and set aside.

Remove the skillet from the heat and pour off the excess fat but do not wipe or scrape the skillet clean. Still off the heat, add the ⅓ cup of cognac and carefully ignite it with a lighter or long match. Gently shake the skillet until the flame dies. Return the skillet to medium heat and add the cream and green peppercorns. Bring the mixture to a boil and whisk for 5 minutes, or until the sauce coats the back of a spoon. Add the teaspoon of cognac and season to taste with salt.

Serve the steaks drizzled with the sauce.

Dauphinoise Potatoes

Serves 4

3 pounds russet potatoes

3 cups heavy cream

4 garlic cloves, smashed with the side of a knife but not chopped

2 sprigs fresh thyme

1 teaspoon kosher salt

1 teaspoon ground black pepper

1 cup fresh breadcrumbs

2 tablespoons extra virgin olive oil

½ cup chopped fresh parsley

You will also need:

aluminum foil

Preheat the oven to 350°F and butter a 9 × 13-inch baking dish.

Peel the potatoes and slice them thinly: about ⅛ inch thick.

Place the cream in a saucepan with the garlic cloves and thyme sprigs, and warm over medium heat for about 3 minutes, until bubbles just begin to form around the edge of the pot. Do not bring to a full boil. Remove from the heat and discard the garlic and thyme.

Ladle a small amount of the cream into the bottom of the baking dish. Add a layer of potatoes, overlapping them slightly and spreading them evenly. Sprinkle with salt and pepper. Ladle over another layer of cream. Repeat with the remaining ingredients, alternating layers of potatoes, salt and pepper, and cream. Pour any excess cream over the top, shaking the dish to distribute the cream evenly.

Cover the dish with foil and bake for 1 hour.

Meanwhile, place the breadcrumbs, olive oil, and parsley in a bowl and combine well.

Remove the dish from the oven, remove the foil, and sprinkle over the breadcrumb mixture. Return the dish to the oven and bake for a further 15 minutes, until the topping is golden. Remove from the oven and cut into squares to serve.

Salad of Mixed Greens, Avocado, and Stilton with Dijon Vinaigrette

A mixed green salad of butter lettuce, baby gems, and baby arugula perfectly stands up to a hearty steak dish. Tossed in a creamy Dijon dressing with clusters of Stilton cheese and avocado, it's practically a meal in itself.

Serves 4

Mixed Greens Salad

small head of bibb lettuce
handful of baby arugula
head of baby gem lettuce

½ large avocado, cut into chunks
2 ounces Stilton cheese, broken
*   into clusters*

Dijon Vinaigrette

2 tablespoons champagne vinegar
½ tablespoon minced shallots
½ tablespoon Dijon mustard

⅓ cup extra virgin olive oil
kosher salt and freshly ground pepper

In a small bowl, whisk the champagne vinegar with the shallot and Dijon mustard. In a thin, steady stream, whisk in the olive oil until emulsified. Season to taste with salt and pepper. Lightly dress the mixed green salad and serve in a bowl for guests to serve themselves.

For an herb vinaigrette
Add ¼ teaspoon each of chopped thyme and chopped tarragon.

For a lemon vinaigrette
Substitute 1½ tablespoons lemon juice for the vinegar and add ¼ teaspoon grated lemon zest.

Chocolate Choux Puff

An elegant dessert that has every bit of the wow factor – crisp golden choux pastry, whipped heavy cream, and a rich chocolate sauce to finish it all off.

Serves 4

Choux Puffs

4 tablespoons unsalted butter
⅔ cup sparkling mineral water
1 level tablespoon granulated sugar

⅓ cup all-purpose flour, sifted onto parchment paper
2 large eggs, lightly beaten

Melt the butter with the sparkling water and sugar in a heavy-based saucepan on a medium-high heat. Bring to a boil, turn off the heat, and add the flour all at once. Beat thoroughly with a wooden spoon until the mixture forms a smooth ball. Turn the ball into a bowl and let cool for 15 minutes.

Preheat the oven to 400°F.

Beat in the eggs, a little at a time, until the mixture is shiny.

Line a sheet pan with parchment paper. Divide the mixture into eight and place on the baking sheet.

Bake for 30 minutes until risen and golden brown and crisp. Turn off the oven. Leave the choux puffs in the oven for 10 minutes then remove and cool on a wire rack.

Filling

1 cup heavy cream   *1 teaspoon granulated sugar*
1 teaspoon vanilla extract

Whip the cream with the vanilla extract and sugar.

Topping

7 ounces dark chocolate   *6 tablespoons unsalted butter*

Melt the chocolate in a bowl over a pan of simmering water, remove from the heat, and stir in the butter until melted and combined.

Halve the cooled puffs and fill with whipped cream. Put the two halves together and top with the chocolate mixture.

CHAPTER SIX

Beaujolais, Picnics, and Children

Different times of year brought different celebrations at Blostin's. In November, it was time to celebrate Beaujolais Nouveau, the fruity red wine from the Beaujolais region of France. The wine is served slightly cooler than red wine usually is and has a shelf life of about six months. If not consumed by then, it can turn flat. A wine for drinking and not keeping! For a French country-style restaurant, creating a menu around the arrival of that year's Beaujolais Nouveau made perfect sense for our customers and our marketing.

In England, there is always the excitement of being able to try the new Beaujolais on the first day of its release and many pub and restaurant owners travel to France to pick up cases for their customers. This was the first year since I'd been there that Blostin's had a Beaujolais Nouveau event. I was especially tuned into this excitement. A race organized by the town to see which restaurant or pub owner would be the first to make it to France and bring the wine back made it even more festive.

This particular year, Bill was teaming up with his friend John from the Strode Arms. They were planning to drive to France and pick up the Beaujolais wine themselves. It was a fun adventure and a way to get some publicity at the same time. There was no prize money, just a friendly contest between competitors in business. It was a small town, and we were all friends.

Monica and I waved goodbye to Bill and John as they started their journey in a Range Rover we packed with food so they could eat on the road. They had thirty-six hours to get there and back. The energy was high in the village and people were making reservations at the participating places to be ready for the homecoming of the teams.

Our menu for the event started out on cocktail napkins. One night over a glass of wine, Bill, Monica, Dennis, and I sat down and created a special prix fixe menu. It was quite a fun, heated collaboration of opinions as we each had our favorite dishes, but in the end we all agreed on the menu selections.

The first course was a choice between French Onion Soup, a Baby Frisée Salad with Lardons, Garlic Croutons, Poached Egg with Truffle Vinaigrette, or a Fresh Salmon Mousse with Cornichons and Brioche Toasts. The entrée was a choice between Grilled Grainy Mustard Steak with Pommes Frites and Tomato Confit (Provençale), Coq au Vin with Buttered Noodles, or Mussels Poached in a Beaujolais Wine with Fennel and Shallots and Grilled Large Garlic French Bread. The final course was a choice of a selection of cheese, Floating Island, or Chocolate Pot de Crème.

To further build excitement among our customers, we put the menu on the blackboard days ahead and also printed a few menu cards, which we thought might help us take orders a little quicker than normal. We were completely sold out for both nights – Friday and Saturday. We even overbooked, because experience told us that we'd get a few last-minute cancellations.

Dennis and I had been dating for a while at this point. He was now established as the "boyfriend" and Bill and John left Dennis, Monica and me to get everything ready for when they crossed the finish line.

In addition, the release of Beaujolais Nouveau that year was November 16, Dennis's birthday, so we had even more to celebrate. There was true excitement in the air once the chefs left for France, as we hustled to get everything ready. This would not be a normal evening in the restaurant. It was as if we were putting on a party. Monica had a banner made to go across the road at the restaurant – this would be the "finish line." Dennis brought a few of his friends to get this done – no easy task, we found out as they precariously hung the banner. It was a wonder none of them fell. But they didn't, and when it was done it looked quite fabulous.

"They've arrived!" Monica shouted as she ran through the restaurant. It was 4:30 p.m. and we opened at 6, so it was all hands on deck to unload the wine and chill some bottles for those who liked to drink it that way. Did Bill and John come first in the race? No, they came in third, but no one cared. All the participants scattered to their various locations to get ready for the evening festivities, as most of them were the chefs and were executing the food themselves that night in their own establishments.

I dressed for the night in a matching black floral blouse and skirt. The skirt had a flare when I turned or did a twirl. I wore black patent leather high heels to accent the look and did my lips in bright red. After all, it was not only the release of the wine, it was also Dennis's birthday, and I wanted to look fabulous for him.

Monica and I worked together as we knew it was going to be extremely busy. Dennis tended to be a fixture at the bar, but that night he helped us greet guests, bid them good night, and lent a hand with anything else that needed to be done for the smooth running of the evening.

The restaurant was so alive that night – it was bustling with laughter, filled with the smell of delicious foods, glasses clinking more than normal. Everyone had come out in a mellow mood to indulge and have a good time.

When the service was finally over, we all collapsed, exhausted but energized, saying goodbye to the last guest as they left the restaurant. I looked at my watch and realized it was just past midnight. Monica lined the glasses on the bar and poured Joseph Drouhin Beaujolais wine. As we picked up our glasses, we all said "Cheers!" and Bill made a little speech. "To friends and family and the love of drinking Beaujolais Nouveau! Happy Birthday, Dennis. We couldn't have done this without you."

We then set up a table in the restaurant laden with food and open bottles of wine, and partied into the night. A birthday candle was placed in the pot de crème for Dennis to make his wish. The next morning, I found out what his birthday wish was.

We were sitting at my favorite morning spot at Blostin's. Behind the kitchen there was a wide flagstone path that stretched all along the terraced building, and on it was a rickety teak table with several wooden café chairs pulled up to it. It wasn't much, but it was charming. There was a little nip in the air, but I had made a French press of roast coffee to keep us warm.

After Dennis took a few sips of coffee, he started, "Peeps," – using his nickname for me – "I would love to meet the children. We've been dating for a while, and getting to know them would make me so happy. What do you think?"

I didn't answer for a long moment, thinking that this would surely change our whole relationship. Perhaps we should just enjoy what we had. My mind continued to race. *I get that he is curious as I do chat about them quite a bit. How could I not? They are so much of my life. But to intertwine them with a stranger could be disruptive to us all. Gosh, I am nattering on here. A meeting together with the children cannot possibly hurt, can it? After all, he's not moving in and living with us, we're just doing lunch. I am overthinking this. We can do lunch, that is OK,* I determined after a whole internal conversation.

I eventually broke the awkward silence, saying, "Why not? I think that would be OK. Let's go out somewhere and have lunch. Next week might work as they're on half term." What was I getting myself into? *It's fine, for God's sake, Pauline, it's only lunch*, I had to keep reminding myself.

"Really? That's wonderful. How about the King's Arms in Litton? They have a garden, swings, and a menu for children," he replied. *Oh, you have it all worked out?* I thought. "The King's Arms is perfect, a great choice," I responded.

Still, I had my doubts. The children were Number One with me and I didn't want to bring anyone emotionally into their lives who would change our dynamic. They already went to and fro with their father and me and, although they tested us both from time to time, overall they had adjusted to the breakup of the marriage very well. David and I were on the same page regarding discipline, and we never spoke ill of each other, which made the transition for the children work.

My last question to myself was if I needed to tell David I was going to introduce Joanne and Ross to the man I'd been dating. My answer: *I don't think so. I have this under control!*

Steamed Mussels in Beaujolais Wine

What's better than steamed mussels poached in Beaujolais wine with garlic, shallots, and fennel? When they come with crispy French fries, of course!

Serves 4

Mussels

1 large shallot, finely chopped

½ cup finely chopped yellow onion

½ cup finely chopped fennel

½ cup Beaujolais wine

½ cup chicken broth

4 tablespoons unsalted butter cut

in ½-inch cubes

1 tablespoon white wine vinegar

4½ pounds of mussels, scrubbed and debearded*

2 tablespoons chopped flat leaf parsley

freshly ground black pepper

Place the shallot, onion, fennel, wine, chicken broth, butter, and vinegar in a large heavy pot. Add the mussels, cover, and bring to a boil. Reduce the heat to low and cook for 3–5 minutes, gently shaking the pot once or twice, until the mussels open. Discard any mussels that don't open. Using a slotted spoon, divide the mussels between 4 bowls and pour over the broth. Sprinkle with chopped parsley and ground black pepper.

*Discard any that are open and don't close when tapped.

Pommes Frites (French Fries)

2 pounds russet potatoes, peeled, rinsed, and dried

4 cups vegetable oil, for frying
kosher salt

Cut the potatoes into sticks approximately 3 inches long. Divide into 4 portions.

Pour the oil into a deep fryer with a basket to reach halfway up the side and heat to 325°F.

Fry each portion of potatoes in the heated oil for 4–5 minutes, until golden but not brown. Remove the basket of fries, turn the fries onto a plate lined with paper towels, and sprinkle with kosher salt. Serve a portion of fries in a ramekin in the center of each bowl of mussels.

Smoked Salmon Cheesecake Mousse

Elegant yet familiar, this creamy smoked salmon cheesecake mousse is my go-to for any cocktail party menu. The addition of a Parmesan crust and fresh dill takes it to the next level of yum.

Serves 8

5 tablespoons grated Parmesan cheese

2 tablespoons fine dried breadcrumbs

2 tablespoons finely chopped fresh dill

3 tablespoons butter

1½ cups chopped white onion

3½ cups cream cheese, softened

4 eggs

⅓ cup heavy cream

½ pound smoked salmon, chopped

½ cup shredded Gruyère cheese

3 tablespoons grated Parmesan cheese

kosher salt and pepper

crackers and crostini, to serve

You will also need:

aluminum foil

Preheat the oven to 350°F.

Lightly butter an 8-inch springform pan. Mix 2 tablespoons of the grated Parmesan with the breadcrumbs and chopped dill. Sprinkle this mixture into the pan, turning and tapping the pan to coat the inside. Wrap a large piece of foil underneath and up the outer sides of the pan.

In a medium skillet, melt the butter over medium heat. Add the chopped onion and sauté for 5 minutes, or until tender. Remove from the heat and let cool. In a large bowl, beat together the cream cheese, eggs, and cream until well blended. Fold in the onions, salmon, Gruyére cheese, and the remaining Parmesan, and season to taste with salt and pepper. Pour into the prepared pan.

Place the wrapped springform pan inside a large roasting pan.

Place in the oven and pour enough boiling water into the roasting pan to come 2 inches up the side of the springform pan.

Bake until firm to the touch, about 1 hour 40 minutes. Carefully remove both pans from the oven and turn off the heat. Lift the springform pan out of the water and return it to the oven. Let stand in the cooling oven for 1 hour. Transfer to a wire rack and let cool completely. Remove from the pan and serve with crackers and crostini.

Floating Island

This classic French dessert is a fluffy meringue floating in a pool of creamy custard finished with threads of caramel. A few steps, but all fairly easy for an intermediate cook. The final result is very impressive and worth the effort!

Serves 6

Meringue

1 ⅔ cups of egg white (about 12 eggs) *1½ cups granulated sugar*
large pinch of salt *1 teaspoon pure vanilla extract*
½ teaspoon cream of tartar

Preheat the oven to 250°F.

Beat the egg whites on a moderate speed until you have a good foam. Beat in the salt and cream of tartar then gradually increase the speed to fast until soft peaks have formed. Beat in the sugar a large spoonful at a time and continue until stiff shiny peaks are formed. Beat in the vanilla.

Form 6 scoops of meringue on a sheet tray lined with parchment. Bake on the lower middle shelf of the oven for about 40 minutes. The meringues will have risen about 3 to 4 inches. Remove from the oven. As the meringues cool, they will sink to their original size. The meringues can be made up to 4 days ahead of time – store in an airtight container.

Crème Anglaise

6 large eggs yolks

2/3 cup granulated sugar

1½ cups very hot milk

1 teaspoon pure vanilla extract

pinch of salt

Whisk the egg yolks in a 2-quart saucepan. Add the sugar by the spoonful – if it goes in all at once, the yolks can turn grainy. Continue beating for 2–3 minutes, until the mixture is pale yellow and thick. Stir in the hot milk in a slow, thin stream. Stir it, rather than beat, so the sauce doesn't foam.

Set the saucepan over a moderate-low heat, stirring with a wooden spoon. Don't overheat as the eggs will scramble. The sauce is ready when it coats the back of the wooden spoon with a light creamy layer, thick enough to hold when you draw your finger across it. Beat in the vanilla extract and a pinch of salt. Set aside to cool.

Caramel

1 cup granulated sugar

⅓ cup water

2–3 tablespoons heavy cream

1 tablespoon butter

Blend the sugar and water in a small saucepan and bring to a simmer. Remove from the heat and swirl the pan by its handle to ensure the sugar has dissolved completely and the liquid is perfectly clear. Cover the pan tightly and boil the syrup for several minutes over a moderately high heat. After a minute or so, uncover the pan and swirl it slowly for a few seconds until the syrup begins to color. Watch it at this stage very carefully so that it doesn't burn. Continue swirling for a few seconds more until it is a light caramel brown, then remove from the heat. Stir in the cream and butter.

It will foam up a bit but just continue stirring. Set the base of the pan in a cold-water bath to stop the cooking and cool the caramel.

To serve, place a few spoonfuls of custard in a shallow bowl and place a meringue in the center. Just before serving, reheat the caramel until you can lift the syrup with a fork and drizzle thin strands over the meringue.

CHAPTER SEVEN

Meeting the Children

It was finally the day the children and I were going to have lunch with Dennis. We were eating breakfast when Joanne asked if she could go to the park. Ross was eating his cornflakes as I sat down next to Joanne with my mug of tea and said, "Today, my darlings, we're going to have lunch with a friend of mine. His name is Dennis. We're going to this pub to have lunch in the garden. They have swings, and we can play hide-and-seek as well."

"Oh," was the response.

"Don't you think that sounds like fun?"

Neither of them seemed too excited at the prospect of meeting whoever this Dennis was. That part of the conversation seemed to go right over their heads. "Swings" and "play hide-and-seek" was what they heard. *Great, let's not put the emphasis on Dennis*, I thought. "So why don't you two go and play for a while. In the meantime, I need to get the restaurant ready for tonight."

They climbed down from the table and ran into the lounge. I felt very fortunate that they played well together and didn't demand my attention all of the time. It always made me smile to watch the dynamic between them. Joanne was the boss, the Chatty

Cathy of the two, while Ross was the quieter one with a shy disposition. He picked his battles, though, and wouldn't be bossed about too much. Joanne was the big sister who was always there to protect him.

Joanne was four and Ross was just three. I couldn't help but think what a perfect age they both were. I could communicate with them, they were curious, and their personalities were forming. Most importantly, they really were fun to be around. *I must enjoy and cherish these times*, I thought. As my dad always said, little babies, little problems, big babies, big problems, and before you know it, they will be all grown up. *So, enjoy it, Pauline*, I said to myself as I ran downstairs to the restaurant.

I got myself ready while Joanne and Ross were playing. It was quite beautiful out and, as always, I liked to feel and look good when going out with Dennis, even though today was different. *This could be interesting*, I thought. *I hope I'm not making a mistake.* I chose to wear my favorite pair of jeans, I put on my light blue polo-necked jumper and my new black Chelsea boots, and then the final touch, my red lipstick.

I told Dennis we would meet him downstairs rather than him coming up to the apartment. I told him no kissing, no holding hands, or any sign of affection during this time with the children. I heard the doorbell. "OK, let's go! Dennis is here, are you ready to have some fun?" I asked them. "Yesss," they yelled back, with a jump in their step as we ran down the stairs.

Joanne was right by my side, not wanting to miss anything as I opened the door. "Hello," Dennis said with a smile as he looked down at her. "What's your name?"

"Joanne," she responded proudly.

"Where's your brother?" he asked. We both looked behind us and there was Ross, hiding behind the door with only his head peeking out.

"Come on, Ross, come and say hello to Dennis," I said. He reluctantly moved forward, looking down at the ground as he walked toward us. He looked up at Dennis, as much as to say, *Who are you?*

"You must be Ross," Dennis said.

Holding my leg, Ross looked up as I implored, "Say hello to Dennis." "Hello," he muttered into my leg. *That is as much as we're going to get out of him at this stage*, I thought.

"OK, off we go," I said, taking Ross's hand. Joanne had already jumped into the car and I lifted Ross in and sat him next to her.

The King's Arms is a fifteenth-century pub in Litton that started life as a flour mill. It was the focal point of the village at that time, located at the foot of the Mendip Hills. It was a quaint and charming pub that had earned a reputation for serving scrumptious food. As we drove into the parking area, we could see the beautifully tended garden that overlooked the valley. There were wooden tables with bench seats attached and a closed parasol in the center. "I hope you have a lot of energy – the children will wear you out on this lunch date," I said, looking around at Dennis.

"I'm up for it," he smiled. "They're very cute, just like their mother."

Right, always the charmer, I thought, nodding my head with a smile.

The children had already decided which table we were going to sit at and they perched themselves on a bench seat.

"Who would like what?" Dennis asked.

"As a treat, would you like apple juice?" I asked the children, and of course they said yes. "I'll have a small shandy, and maybe you can bring out the menu. I'll stay and watch Joanne and Ross." *Oh my, the mother in me is taking over here*, I thought to myself.

Lunch was a mixture of chaos, loudness, and fun. The children were themselves and seemed to be OK with Dennis in their presence. We played on the swings, with Dennis and me pushing them as high as we could as neither of them had any fear of this. We played hide-and-seek and I helped Ross and Joanne find hiding places from Dennis. Neither of them could keep quiet and they would giggle while waiting for him to find them as he shouted out "Where are you?" Then he would creep up to them with a big "Boo! I found you!" and they would scream and run off again. He was a natural with the children, maybe because he's one of six children and he has three younger brothers.

We left the children to play while we ordered lunch. This place had a reputation for good simple food, which was just what we needed with the children, nothing too fussy. We ordered sausage and chips for Joanne and Ross. I decided on the brussels sprout, broccoli, and leek quiche with a sprinkle of Stilton cheese. Dennis went for the Shepherd's Pie.

Sipping on my shandy, I looked at Dennis and asked, "Would you ever want children?"

"I'd love to have children. Up until now, I hadn't found the right person. I'm from a big family and I can't think of anything better than having children in my life." And with that the food arrived, and I was left thinking about his answer. Joanne and Ross came running to the table.

Wow, I was not expecting this, I thought, as I surveyed the food we'd ordered. The pork sausage was big and fat and had been butterflied, with a sage sprig for garnish. A little stainless-steel jug with some pork gravy to pour over came with it. The fries were more like steak fries – they were hand cut, sprinkled with salt and vinegar, and served in a cone on its side on the plate. All of this was completely wasted on Joanne and Ross, but it looked delicious and appetizing. I cut up the sausage for Ross, at the same time taking a bite to taste. "Mmm, that's nice, Ross, you'll like it," I said, while Dennis cut the sausage for Joanne. *Just like a happy family*, I thought.

They had also brought us linen napkins, which are out of character for pub food but such a nice touch. I was surprised by the appearance of a half-bottle of Crozes Hermitage red wine and looked up at Dennis. He understood exactly what my look meant. "I thought it would be nice to have a glass of wine with lunch," he said, glancing at me for approval. *Would it be OK to have a glass with the children? Yes, it would*, and I simply said, "Fabulous, I love a Rhône wine."

My quiche was not just a slice but an individual serving with a nice thick crust, topped with some arugula glistening with a light dressing of olive oil and lemon. I had no expectations – one never knows with pub food – but it looked delicious. I looked across at the Shepherd's Pie Dennis had ordered. It was served in a small black skillet. It looked great and I noticed that the mashed potatoes were piped on in circles, like a dart board, rather than plopped on.

I reached across to put my fork in his pie to taste. Dennis put his hand up as much as to say, *Wait, let me taste first*. I stopped myself and sort of laughed, knowing that it had become a bad habit of mine since we'd been dating. I always seemed to take the first taste of the sauce or whatever intrigued me on Dennis's plate before he got to taste, and without asking. He looked at me with a smile and then he took a forkful of the pie and served it to me. I savored the taste – large chunks of lamb in a rich sauce that had a hint of mint flavor, and the creaminess of the mashed potatoes made it taste divine. "It's wonderful, I love the twist of adding the mint."

Dennis tried to make polite table conversation with a three- and a four-year-old. "Where do you live?" Joanne asked Dennis as she was eating her chips. "Not far from you. I can walk to Blostin's from my house. Maybe you can come and see it one day," he said. She didn't answer and continued eating. Ross just kept focused and ate his lunch. Both were good eaters and would eat most things, which was a blessing as I never had to cook alternative meals for them.

"Wow, where did the time go? We need to leave." I got up and began packing our things away. "I have to work tonight. Let's go to the bathroom before we leave," I said to the children.

"I can take Ross," Dennis said.

I hesitated. They did seem quite comfortable with him, but was Ross ready to venture alone with Dennis with me out of sight? I made a quick decision, just in case Ross decided he did not want to go with Dennis and made a scene, and said, "It's OK, I'm quite used to handling both of them." I smiled, took their hands, and walked inside the pub, looking for the toilets. Dennis was waiting for us by the car when we were done.

When we arrived at Blostin's, Dennis let the children out of the back seat. I opened the restaurant door to let them in. "Children, what do you say to Dennis? You need to thank him for your lunch," I said. "Thank you," said Joanne in a bright cheerful way, whereas Ross kept his head down and could barely mutter the words. With that, they both ran through the restaurant and I could hear them running up the stairs.

Dennis walked closer to me and, looking into my eyes, said, "You have two very special children."

"They aren't too bad," I said, looking at the floor and suddenly feeling a little shy. I underplayed the compliment and with a slight laugh added, "It truly was a nice lunch. I think the children were having fun with you as they let you play with them. Hopefully they ran around enough so that they'll sleep soundly tonight."

"Well, I must admit this is a first for me. I've never gone out to lunch with a date and her children. I can see it is quite exhausting," he said, laughing. "I'd like to think we could do it again though."

I didn't answer his question but was thinking, *you never know.* But I didn't say that. Instead, I surprised myself and said, "We're not very busy tonight. Would you like to come by after service?" He paused and nodded and then stepped away. *That must be because of my no-kissing rule*, I thought. He smiled and said, walking to his car, "I can't wait to see you," and with that he blew me a kiss and drove away.

I watched him until his car was out of sight. I lingered in the same spot for a moment and thought, *OK, Pauline, I do believe that went well. I enjoyed being with him and the children. It felt natural.*

As I went into the restaurant, I heard Bill calling from the kitchen. "Where have you been? Have you been out with Dennis?" he teased.

"None of your business," I said, laughing as I passed him, heading to the stairs to my apartment.

"He's a good chap, you know that, right?" he yelled out.

Yes, I know that, I said to myself, smiling, as I went into the apartment and closed the door behind me.

Shepherd's Pie

This is one of those go-to dishes for every busy mum in England. It's delicious with chunky lamb cooked with onions, sweet peas, and carrots in a velvety lamb gravy, topped with creamy golden mashed potatoes.

Serves 6

1½ pounds russet potatoes

1 stick unsalted butter, softened

salt and pepper

2 tablespoons olive oil

1 cup chopped onion

2 large carrots, peeled and diced small

2 garlic cloves, chopped

1½ pounds ground lamb

2 tablespoons all-purpose flour

2 teaspoons tomato paste

1 cup chicken broth

1 cup fresh or frozen English peas

kosher salt and pepper

Peel the potatoes and cut into ½-inch dice. Place in a medium saucepan and cover with cold water. Cover and bring to a boil over high heat, then uncover, reduce the heat to a simmer, and cook for 10–15 minutes, until tender and easily crushed with tongs. Drain the potatoes in a colander and return to the saucepan. Mash the potatoes with softened butter, season to taste with salt and pepper, and mash until smooth.

Preheat the oven to 400°F.

While the potatoes are cooking, prepare the filling. Place the olive oil in a 12-inch skillet and set over medium-high heat. Once the oil shimmers, add the onions and carrots and sauté for 3–4 minutes, just until they begin to take color. Stir in the garlic. Add the lamb, sprinkle with the flour, and toss to coat, continuing to cook for another minute. Stir in the tomato paste and chicken broth. Bring to a boil, reduce the heat to low, cover, and simmer slowly for 10–12 minutes, or until the sauce is thickened slightly. Remove from the heat.

Add the peas to the mixture, season to taste with salt and pepper, and spread in a 9 × 9-inch glass baking dish. Top with the mashed potatoes. Place on the middle shelf and bake for 25 minutes, or until the potatoes begin to brown. Remove to a cooling rack for 15 minutes before serving.

Pancetta, Leek, and Brussels Sprout Quiche

I love serving quiche in individual tart pans rather than having one large pie. It brings this lovely dish to the next level, as do the crispy pancetta, brussels sprouts, and leeks in this version. Serve with a tossed green salad and you have the makings of a perfect breakfast, lunch, or even dinner.

Serves 4

Crust

2½ cups all-purpose flour, plus extra for dusting

½ teaspoon salt

3 sticks unsalted butter, cubed

¼ cup plus 3 tablespoons ice water

You will also need:

plastic wrap

aluminum foil

pie weights or dried beans

In a food processor, pulse the flour with the salt. Add the butter and pulse until it is the size of small peas. Add the ice water and pulse until the pastry is moistened. Turn the pastry out onto a floured work surface and knead 2 or 3 times, just until smooth. Pat the pastry into 4 disks, cover with plastic wrap, and refrigerate until firm, about 20 minutes.

Preheat the oven to 375°F.

On the floured surface, roll 1 pastry disk into a 6-inch round. Ease the pastry without stretching into a 4-inch fluted tart pan with a removable bottom. Trim the excess and use it to patch any holes. Repeat with the remaining pastry disks. Refrigerate the tart shells for 10 minutes.

Line the tart shells with foil, fill with pie weights, and blind bake for 30 minutes, just until dry. Remove the foil and pie weights and bake the shells for a further 15 minutes, until they are dry and golden. Transfer the tart pans to a baking sheet.

Filling

1 pound thickly sliced pancetta,
  roughly diced
3 large leeks, white and tender green
  parts only, thinly sliced
8 brussels sprouts, tough outer leaves
  removed, thinly sliced
1 teaspoon chopped thyme leaves

1 cup shredded Gruyère cheese
4 large eggs
2 large egg yolks
2½ cups heavy cream
kosher salt and freshly ground
  black pepper

In a large skillet, cook the pancetta over a moderately high heat, stirring, for about 7 minutes, until browned and crisp. Drain the pancetta, leaving the fat in the pan. Add the leeks, brussels sprouts, and thyme to the skillet, season to taste with salt and pepper, and cook over a moderate heat, stirring occasionally, for about 5 minutes, until the leeks are softened but not browned. Transfer to a bowl and let cool. Stir in the pancetta and the Gruyère cheese.

In a bowl, whisk the eggs with the egg yolks and heavy cream. Stir in the pancetta mixture and season to taste with salt and pepper. Divide the custard evenly between the tart shells and bake for about 30 minutes, rotating the sheet halfway through for even baking, until puffed and lightly browned. Transfer the quiches to a rack and let cool for 15 minutes. Remove from the rings and serve warm.

CHAPTER EIGHT

Dinner at a Castle

"So, about tonight ..." We were on our way to dinner with my younger sister Angela and her husband, Graham. As we drove along the country lanes to Thornbury Castle, Dennis mused, "Can I expect the third degree over Beef Wellington?"

I laughed, but he wasn't too far off the truth. I was in no rush to have him meet the family for precisely that reason, but Angie had caught me off guard by calling the restaurant during my shift. I picked up the phone, thinking it was someone wanting to make a reservation. Instead, I heard my sister... "Why have Mum and Dad met Dennis and not me?" I'd introduced Dennis to my parents on a whim when he and I were returning from a trip together. Now, rolling my eyes, I had to smile. It was so her. She always wanted to be in the know.

"Oh, she's better than any MI5 interrogator," I laughed, answering Dennis. "She'll extract all she wants to know. But you can handle her. She has a heart of gold and has the best interest for us all. Plus, she's a lot of fun and has a great sense of humor. Besides, you already have the seal of approval from my parents."

Leaving Somerset, we'd taken a route through all the

countryside villages to avoid Bristol city traffic. We sped along the River Avon, over beautiful miles of green grass, known as the Downs, then on to the A38, a two-lane road that wound its way through many small villages bordered by gray stone walls. It eventually led us into Thornbury, a small market town in the county of Gloucestershire. Thornbury's high street was cobbled and lined with charming small boutique, family-owned businesses. Many of the buildings were Tudor in architecture.

As we got to the end of the high street, the castle grounds came into view. Marking the entrance were two gray stone pillars crowned with small decorative turrets. On one side of the pillars was a gray stone wall that enclosed the grounds for as far as we could see, and on the other was a gray stone gatehouse with a steeply pitched slate tile roof. The only sign was a small brass plaque in one of the pillars, etched with the name Thornbury Castle. "Here it is," I shouted out, as we were about to miss the entrance.

The entire experience of arriving there was like something out of a movie. An arch of trees lined the graveled road. Around one more bend and then, "Wow!" Before our eyes was a huge open space. On one side of the car was a massive lush green lawn and on the other were rows of grapevines. Straight ahead was a large stone archway that took us into the inner courtyard of the castle, with a large square lawn in the middle. "Wow," I said again.

As we parked, I spotted Angela and Graham's car. "Here we go, hopefully I pass the test," Dennis said. "You'll be just fine. I want her to like you, but I'm the one that needs to approve of you, not her." We both smiled and relaxed a bit as I put my arm through his.

Thornbury Castle dates back to 1510 with some sections dating as far back as 1330. King Henry VIII, being of a covetous nature, had the owner, the 3rd Duke of Buckingham, beheaded for treason and then confiscated his castle. He then stayed there with Anne Boleyn for their honeymoon. The castle remained the property of the crown for a few decades, but although it was then returned to the duke's family, it remained unoccupied for two centuries until, in 1850, it was partially renovated as a family home.

Now it was owned by Kenneth Bell MBE (Member of the Order of the British Empire). Mr. Bell was a restaurateur who had bought the castle in 1966 and lived there with his family. He turned the main area into a one-Michelin-star Relais & Châteaux restaurant.

The massive arched wooden door into the castle was impressive, with carved panels decorated with iron studs. Dennis pressed down the huge iron lever on the door, which led us into the reception area. An uneven flagstone floor with a suit of armor on one side and a large grandfather clock on the other took us right back in time.

Angela and Graham were sitting in a circular alcove paneled in dark wood. Above the paneled walls, 12-foot-high rounded beveled windows were connected by stone casings. The ceilings were about 20 feet high, with beautiful detailed wooden beams. A fire roared next to them. They had picked the perfect table.

Dennis and I looked at each other and gave a sigh. We were completely in awe of our surroundings. "This is something," Dennis said, as he put his hand in mine.

They stood up immediately as we approached them. Angela held out her hand to Dennis. "So you're the mystery man we've all wanted to meet!" Graham shook Dennis's hand with a knowing smile.

Angela had already ordered us all the house specialty, Kir Royales. As we settled into our seats, the waiter brought us menus and small plates of food he called "tapas." We looked as if we needed more explanation, and he obliged. "It's a traditional dish they serve in Spain, my home country." I hadn't seen tapas served yet anywhere and was excited to try something new.

As the men settled in, Angela did that thing all women do – asked me to go to the powder room with her. I knew what she wanted – all the juicy details – but I got in the first question as we walked through the grand halls flanked with more suits of armor and tapestries from a thousand lifetimes ago. "So, what did Mum and Dad think of Dennis?"

"They said he was charming, a gentleman, and that the two of you seemed pretty comfortable with each other. They liked him. Is he the one?" she asked outright.

"Come on, Ang, how do I know? All I know is we have a lot of fun together. There's no way I'm going to commit to anyone straight away. Only time will tell, and I'm in no hurry. To answer your question of why he met Mum and Dad first..." I had to admit, I quite enjoyed heading her off at the pass. "It was just a last-minute thing. We were coming back from a trip to Tunisia and their house was on the way."

Uncharacteristically, Angie stopped the conversation by holding up one hand. "I want to hear all about it, but let's order dinner first and then we can relax, and you can tell both Graham and me about your exotic affair. That way, I won't have to repeat it to him later," she said, laughing.

Back at the table, Angela, the take-charge girl, suggested we order the restaurant's famous dishes. She ordered Salmon en Croûte, and for starters, the Artichoke Salad and Avocado with Shrimp and Dill Aioli.

"Cheers," I said, picking up my Kir Royale. Angela and Graham had been married for about ten years. It truly was young love, with all the drama that comes with that. Graham was five years older than Angela and wasn't immediately accepted into the family. As soon as Angela turned eighteen and didn't need parental permission, they married. With Graham officially family, things went smoother for them.

"Soooo," said Angela, now in full interrogation mode, "tell us all about Tunisia!" But before we could start that story, the waiter came and took us to our dining table in the Tower Room.

The room was just what you'd imagine from a place where kings and queens had dined. Its walls were covered in rich dark-wood paneling. The ceiling was crowned with beautiful thick beams. The windows around the room were angled, with a deep stone shelf, bringing just enough light and shadow into the room. All this was enhanced by candlelight from iron sconces on the walls and a huge chandelier hung majestically from the center of the beams.

"Not bad, Ang," I said as the waiter pulled out my chair. Graham had already ordered the wine, a Pouilly Fuissé, and Dennis raised his glass. "Thank you for this lovely invitation to dinner. It's wonderful to meet you. I've met your parents, Joanne and Ross, and now you, who I thought I was never going to meet." Then, looking at Angela, he said, "I adore your sister and to meet her family is such a pleasure, so cheers and thank you again." Angela glanced at me with a nod of approval. Dennis had passed.

As we ate, drank, and chatted nonstop, I could not help but be aware of the luxury and history surrounding me. I realized I loved all this more than I knew and felt a surge of contentment and happiness just being in these surroundings. I was in the early stages of following a career in hospitality, and to think when I went to Blostin's that first time, it had never even crossed my mind as a possibility. I wasn't even sure what it entailed. I'd been set up for a working life as a secretary and here I was now, living a life rich with food and wine, with Dennis to enjoy it all with.

My thoughts were interrupted by someone who had come up to the table. It was Kenneth Bell, wondering how we had enjoyed our dinner. It didn't take long for me to realize how special it was to have a Michelin-star restaurateur talking to us at our table. We smiled, slightly taken aback that he was there, and muttered,

"It was delicious, thank you." *I mean, what else would we have said,* I thought later.

"Have you decided what you might like for dessert?" he asked as he gestured to our waiter to present the dessert menu. We were all a bit speechless at the unexpected interlude of meeting the owner. "Please, I'd like you to enjoy dessert with the compliments of the house," he said. I eventually opened my mouth and said, "That's very generous of you, thank you. Is there something you would recommend?"

As he talked, I had some time to observe and wonder about him. He came across perhaps a little arrogant, or was that confidence? He had a big mop of gray hair that he'd push his hand through every now and then to keep it off his forehead. He had a pale complexion and, as he was talking, he would sort of glance down and speak quietly, as if losing his train of thought. Then he would suddenly lift his head and come out with a funny comment in a louder voice, keeping us engaged in what he was talking about.

I ordered the Almond Honey Tart with Blueberries. I knew I wanted it as soon as he mentioned it. He nodded. "Great choice, and if it's OK with you, I'll be back and join you for a glass of Muscat Beaumes de Venise dessert wine."

"What a surprise," Graham said as Mr. Bell walked away. "I wonder what made him come to our table?" Dessert arrived and, true to his word, Mr. Bell arrived with it. He pulled up a chair with a bottle of wine in hand and refreshed all our glasses. *He refilled the glasses without even asking if we wanted more,* I thought, impressed. Mr. Bell began the conversation. "Now, tell me all about yourselves. What brings you to Thornbury Castle?"

By this time, the Tower Restaurant was empty except for us. We were all engaged and more relaxed and felt more comfortable sharing details about ourselves. Mr. Bell told us everything we wanted to know about the castle. We also found out that he had recently divorced, had three children, and that he wanted to expand the castle to be a hotel and not just a restaurant.

The waiter brought us espresso and a special fudge made at the castle, with a cheese plate and some port.

"Bring your glasses. I'd like to show you the wine cellar." As he got up, Mr. Bell went on to say to our waiter, "Fernando, it's late, why don't you call it a night? I'll take care of our guests and lock up."

"Thank you, Mr. Bell. Good night, ladies and gentlemen. I hope to see you again sometime."

We followed Mr. Bell out. He walked up to a large wooden door with iron studs and opened it using a somewhat rusted key. As he pushed it open, I could smell a mustiness. He switched on the light to reveal uneven flagstones and those same gray stone arched walls we had seen throughout the tower. On one wall there was a makeshift wooden structure filled with wine bottles and stone bins containing more wine.

As we got deeper into the cellar, the ceilings got lower. We had to bend down to go through the stone arches. On either side of us were many boxes of all different kinds of wine, and there were loose bottles here and there covered in cobwebs and dust. It was completely out of a movie.

As we walked around the cellar, Dennis and I could not help but notice the names and vintages on the bottles. There were some amazing wines. Dennis whispered in my ear, "This is like I'm having a wine orgasm, this is unbelievable." I laughed, nodding in complete agreement. Fittingly, Mr. Bell admitted he was obsessed with wine.

At one point, we all noticed the time. "It's one in the morning," Angela exclaimed. "My babysitter will wonder where we are." But Mr. Bell had one more surprise for us.

"Before you leave, let me make you some onion soup and

bread." He had a presence that you just did not argue with, and with that we all followed him to the restaurant kitchen.

He went into the walk-in refrigerator and brought out a large container of what we could see was onion soup as he poured it into the saucepan. He told me to get the soup bowls off the shelf. Then he said to Angela, "You'll find spoons in that drawer over there. Please get that basket of bread rolls from the windowsill. Now, ladies, you can take all that out to the restaurant through that door over there," he said, pointing to a swing door. Dennis and Graham just looked on, watching the action and saying nothing, and then followed us out to the restaurant. "I'll bring the soup and ladle," Mr. Bell shouted after us.

He had also opened a bottle of Châteauneuf-du-Pape that was already on the table with glasses. A true host, he must have had Fernando do that before he left, I thought. With his back to the swinging kitchen door, he pushed it open with his body as he was holding a large white tureen filled with the soup. "I hope you like onion soup," he said as he filled all the bowls.

It had been a decadent evening of hospitality. We were not going to forget this night very easily. We all said thank you in a million ways, talking over each other as we spilled out the front door of the castle, shaking his hand good night as we walked toward our cars. "Are you sure we can't help clean up?" I asked. "No! No! Home you go. It's late. Drive carefully, it was nice meeting you all." He stood by the door, waving.

I glanced at my watch. It was 2:30 a.m. "Well, I never saw the evening going in this direction. How unexpected. Why do you think he came over to our table?" I asked. Angela leaned over to give me a hug good night, adding, "We'll analyze this later. Right now, we need to get home." She hugged both Dennis and me at the same time, saying to me with a wink, "You've got a good one, Pauline."

Dennis and Graham did a man hug and Graham gave me a kiss and a hug, whispering, "He's a keeper, don't let him go." And with that, Dennis had received the double seal of approval.

Two weeks after our evening at Thornbury Castle, I got a call. It was Mr. Bell. "Pauline, I would like to offer you a job as Assistant Manager. Would you be interested? Let me know when we can meet to go over the details," he said.

I found myself speechless as I got off the phone. Did he just offer me a job? Or was I imagining it? Once more, the unexpected had happened, just like when I started at Blostin's.

Shrimp Artichoke Avocado Salad

This is my take on Thornbury Castle's famous salad. Sautéed shrimp served with garlic, parsley, and artichokes on a carpaccio of avocado is a beautiful combination of flavors.

Serves 6

6 medium artichokes

juice of one lemon

3 tablespoons extra virgin olive oil, plus extra for drizzling

1 tablespoon chopped parsley

3 large garlic cloves, chopped

1 tablespoon unsalted butter

24 jumbo shrimp, peeled and deveined

¼ cup dry white wine

3 large avocados

kosher salt and black pepper

cracked black pepper

Trim the artichokes to the base, removing any tough outer leaves. Cut away the heart of the choke. Cut each choke head in 8 and place in a bowl. Toss with the lemon juice and cover with water. Set aside for 15 minutes, then drain the artichoke pieces.

Heat half the oil in a heavy skillet over medium heat. Add the artichokes, parsley, and garlic, reduce the heat to low, and cook, stirring from time to time, for about 15 minutes, until the artichokes are lightly browned and tender when pierced with a sharp knife. Remove from the skillet and let cool.

Add the remaining olive oil and the butter to the skillet and add the shrimp. Season to taste with salt and pepper, then add the white wine and cook until the shrimp turns pink and lightly browned on the outside. Let cool.

To serve, peel the avocados and remove the stones. Thinly slice the avocados and arrange the slices around the perimeter of the plates. Place the cooked artichokes in the center and spoon cooled shrimp over the artichoke mixture. Drizzle a little olive oil over the avocado and finish with salt and cracked black pepper to taste.

Whole Salmon En Croûte

Yet another of the Thornbury's signature dishes. Our first time there, we ordered this and the Artichoke Salad to start and enjoyed them both with the restaurant's famous Kir Royale.

Serves 8

Spinach Filling

1 pound spinach
2 tablespoons extra virgin olive oil
2 finely chopped shallots
2 finely chopped large garlic cloves
splash of white wine
juice of ½ lemon

½ cup crème fraîche
¼ cup freshly grated Parmigiano Reggiano cheese
¼ cup toasted breadcrumbs
kosher salt and cracked black pepper

Wash and stem the spinach. Bring a pan of salted water to a boil and place a strainer in the sink and an ice water bath in a large bowl on the counter. Cook the spinach for 1–2 minutes, until just wilted, then strain. Add to the ice bath to shock it. Drain, then wring out the excess liquid in a clean dish towel. Chop the spinach.

Heat the olive oil in a skillet over medium heat. Add the shallots and garlic, and season to taste with salt and pepper. Add the wine and let it absorb. Add the chopped spinach, lemon juice, crème fraîche, Parmigiano, and breadcrumbs. Remove from the heat and let cool.

Salmon and Pastry

1 tablespoon room temperature butter

2 tablespoons Dijon mustard

2 tablespoons chopped fresh dill

2 sheets store-bought puff pastry,
  defrosted in refrigerator for 2 hours

1 side (8–10 pounds) skinless salmon

1 egg

2 teaspoons cold water

kosher salt and freshly ground
  black pepper

Preheat the oven to 425°F, with the rack centered in the oven.

Combine the butter, mustard, and dill in a bowl and set aside. Roll out the puff pastry sheets on a lightly floured surface.

Season the salmon with salt and pepper to taste. Place the salmon on one sheet of pastry and coat with the mustard mixture and then the spinach mixture.

Beat the egg and water with a fork. Lay the second sheet of pastry over the salmon, trim to the shape of the fish, and seal the edges with the end of a teaspoon. Brush the pastry with the egg wash. With a spoon, imprint a fish-scale design on the pastry. Using the pastry trimmings, cut out a small circle of pastry for the eye and a strip of pastry for the mouth and attach with egg wash.

Bake in the oven for 20–25 minutes, until the pastry is golden.

Almond Honey Blueberry Tart

This seems like such a simple dessert for a place like Thornbury Castle, but it's actually the perfect ending to a rich meal. I love the almond crumb topped with fresh blueberries, a swirl of honey, and a fresh mint garnish.

Serves 4

Pastry Shell (Pâté sucrée)

1½ cups all-purpose flour
¼ cup granulated sugar
½ teaspoon fine salt
½ cup cold unsalted butter, cut into pieces

1 large egg yolk
1–2 tablespoons ice water

You will also need:
plastic wrap

Almond Base

½ cup toasted sliced almonds
½ cup white sugar

1 tablespoon all-purpose flour

To serve

12 ounces of fresh large blueberries

1 teaspoon powdered sugar

1 tablespoon of honey

fresh mint sprigs

In a bowl, blend together the flour, sugar, and salt and place in a processor. Add the cold butter pieces and pulse the mixture until it resembles coarse meal.

Add the egg yolk. Add 1 tablespoon of ice water and pulse to form a dough (if necessary to achieve this, add more ice water, a little at a time). Take the dough out of the bowl and flatten into a smooth disc. Cover with plastic wrap and chill in the refrigerator for a minimum of 2 hours.

Let the dough rest at room temperature for 15 minutes before rolling out.

Remove the plastic wrap and, on a lightly floured surface, roll out the dough to fit a 10-inch tart pan (or four 4-inch tart pans). Lay the dough in the tart pan and press it firmly against the base and sides without stretching it. Trim off any excess dough. Cover and chill the dough in the pan for at least 30 minutes before filling and baking.

Preheat the oven to 325°F.

To make the almond base, grind all the ingredients together in a food processor to a fine meal.

Spread the almond base evenly over the base of the tart shell. Place in the oven and bake for about 40 minutes, until the crust begins to get a golden color. Remove the tart from the oven and let cool completely.

To serve, cover the almond base with the blueberries. Dust with the powdered sugar, swirl with the honey, and garnish with fresh mint sprigs.

French Onion Soup

We finished our memorable meal with a bowl of this soup at 2 a.m. Not conventional, but then neither was Kenneth Bell, the owner of Thornbury at the time. He was an enthusiast of this classic soup with its caramelized onions cooked with red wine, beef broth, and herbs, and topped with French baguette slices with Gruyère cheese.

Serves 6

Onion Soup

1 stick unsalted butter
4 large yellow onions, sliced
2 garlic cloves, minced
2 bay leaves
2 sprigs fresh thyme
1 cup red wine

3 heaping tablespoons all-purpose flour
2 quarts beef broth
kosher salt and freshly ground black pepper

Melt the butter in a large pot over medium heat. Add the onions, garlic, bay leaves, and thyme, season to taste with salt and pepper, and cook for about 25 minutes, until the onions are very soft and caramelized. Add the wine and bring to a boil, then reduce the heat and simmer for about 5 minutes, until the wine has evaporated and the onions are dry. Discard the bay leaves and thyme sprigs. Dust the onions with the flour and give them a stir. Turn the heat down to medium-low so the flour does not burn and cook for 10 minutes to cook out the raw taste of the flour.

Add the beef broth, bring the soup back to a simmer, and cook for 10 minutes. Season to taste with salt and pepper.

Topping

1 baguette, sliced   *1 cup shredded Gruyère cheese*

Arrange the baguette slices on a baking sheet in a single layer. Sprinkle the slices with the Gruyère cheese and broil until bubbly and golden brown.

To serve, ladle the soup into bowls and top with the cheesy baguette slices.

CHAPTER NINE

Two Proposals

It was not a normal interview, but then I knew no different. I was invited to dinner at Thornbury Castle to have a conversation about the possibility of working there. Since it was the same interview process at Blostin's, I wondered whether this was how it was done in this industry – over dinner and a glass of wine. If so, I was all for it.

When I arrived, the restaurant was full. This time I was more aware of the activity, seeing it all through the eyes of someone who might be working here.

Dinner was just me and Mr. Bell (I never would be comfortable calling him Kenneth). He'd already chosen the meal and wine, just as you would do if you invited someone to your home. I was intoxicated by all the opportunities that he spoke about and what my role would be. He was about to start the expansion to the castle, he revealed, to become not only a restaurant but a seven-bedroom hotel.

Before dessert, he took me on a tour of the property, through the areas where the rooms would be. His excitement was infectious, and I began to think of all the possibilities for the hotel and for me. It was all spectacular as I climbed up stone spiral staircases, viewed the raw spaces that would become the rooms, and learned more of the history from Mr. Bell.

I'm not sure what he saw in me. Perhaps the same thing Monica and Bill did – a passion for food and wine, a personality that loves people, and a willingness to try anything and be the best I could be at it.

Talking with Mr. Bell, I was definitely more confident than I had been that first night at Blostin's. My role there had morphed into managing all aspects of the restaurant as well as banking and bookkeeping. Although I had never trained as a chef, I was a really good cook and would always assist if chefs were sick or on vacation. In this way, I knew in my heart that I had some talent and, more importantly, the sheer will to make it work. It made me feel very secure as I chatted with Mr. Bell.

Over dessert and coffee, Mr. Bell began talking about my compensation. It was his idea that I live at the castle. He would convert the gatehouse into an apartment for me and the children and he would like me to start sooner rather than later. I knew it would be another upheaval, but I didn't give it further thought. I was so sure I could work it all out and it would all fall into place. I accepted the position that evening. My only request was that I could take a moment to work out the logistics with Blostin's, the place where I had found my passion for hospitality. I had been there for nearly two years and I owed them that much.

But the dynamics there were changing. Bill and Monica's marriage was now in question, and they had raised the possibility of selling the restaurant. They had mentioned that I could potentially stay on with the new owners, so while I hadn't been looking to go somewhere new, the timing of this new opportunity to move on made it easier for me to tell Bill and Monica. We had all become emotionally attached to each other and were like family by this time. So for me to move and be in a good place before they sold the restaurant was comforting to them.

With all these details out of the way, I took a deep breath to absorb it all. Two years earlier, I didn't have a career, much less a guiding passion. Now I'd found a deep love of hospitality and was taking a huge step from a small bistro to a Michelin-star restaurant, soon to be a hotel. I could not help but think about all this as I began to pack up our life above the restaurant. "Wow, Pauline," I said out loud as I wrapped up my favorite wine glasses, "this is something. This is all meant to be."

With all this going on, I had completely managed to ignore the signs that Dennis was getting more serious. We were now regulars at a darling restaurant in Bath called Le Beaujolais. With a name like that, how could we not love it? It was a small, romantic place, family-owned and intimate, not unlike Blostin's.

One evening we settled down at our usual table, ordered our wine, and were told to wait for the chef, who would surprise us with something special for dinner. We were such regulars, we really got to know the chef owner and his team, and it was all quite fabulous to be treated as VIPs and to have some inspirational food cooked by the chef especially for us.

Dennis picked up his glass, took a sip, and with a deep breath he leaned across the table. "I've been thinking, my house is now completely renovated. As you know, it has three bedrooms and I thought it might be wonderful if you and the children could move in with me. I know that Rich is living there with me now, but he's about to move out. What do you think?"

I was stunned into silence. Why had I not seen this coming?

A few years back, Dennis had bought a rundown eighteenth-century terraced house, which he had been renovating and living in ever since I had known him. He had painstakingly restored it to its natural beauty, and I'd watched it come alive under his care.

I had to admit, it would be quite a perfect living arrangement for the children, Dennis, and myself.

But I didn't say that. Instead, I retorted, "Really? You want me and the children to simply move in with you?" I wasn't sure why I reacted like that. I saw his face, stopped to process what he had just asked me, and added in a softer tone, "I just can't do that, I'm so sorry."

Talk about bursting his bubble. He had obviously not made the decision to ask me lightly, especially because his parents and two of his brothers had made it very clear to him that he would be a fool to marry me and take on two children. He probably didn't expect me to respond with such an acidic comment.

He pushed himself back in the chair and I sat across the table holding a glass of champagne in both hands, wondering what had made me respond so harshly. And wondering what would happen next.

Thank goodness the awkward silence was broken as the waiter served a beef carpaccio salad. We ate silently until I couldn't stand it any longer. I needed to explain my reasoning. I put down my knife and fork, brought my hands together, put my elbows on the table, and leaned forward as he had done moments before.

I looked him in the eyes, and he looked back at me. "I am truly sorry. I hadn't meant for that to come out so nastily. I was taken aback. As much as I love being with you, and the children are always excited to see you – after all, you're the best horse they've ever had to play with," – I smiled and he chuckled at all the times he had played "horse" with them – "I'm just not ready to take the next step in our relationship. Please be patient. For me, it just feels too soon. I'm not prepared to commit to another man and go into another relationship that possibly could go bad. I need time."

He listened to what I said, obviously a little hurt. What I had learned about Dennis is that he doesn't do things without absolutely thinking them through. He is that chap who, when he wants to buy something will go to the shop twice before making up his mind, returning the third time when he's decided he's ready to buy. And here he was asking a divorcee with two children to be part of his life. That is a lot to take on. We had already had the discussion that I truly did not want more children, so if we were to become husband and wife then the notion of him having his own biological children would not be fulfilled. I wondered if he would be OK with that.

"I do want to marry you," he said. "I love you, but I thought it might be a good idea to at least move in together, taking it one step at a time."

I looked at him and gave him a big smile, hoping it would make him feel better. Yes, my feelings for him were strong, but was it love? I needed to make sure, and said, "Darling, let's enjoy what we have. It is quite fabulous. It feels free and loving and in my heart of hearts I don't ever want what we have together to come to an end. But for the time being, shall we just enjoy without the commitment?"

He looked at me sadly, but he smiled back and said, "You know I love you, right?"

"Yes, I know," I replied, and then we kissed each other across the table.

As if they had been waiting on the sidelines watching the whole episode, feeling a little embarrassed, the chef and waiter came to the table with our dinner, which was perfect timing.

We dined on poached monkfish with root vegetables, finished with crispy shaved leeks and a fish broth poured tableside. We drank Puligny Montrachet Premier Cru and, putting aside the topic of marriage for the moment, indulged in food and wine as we always did. That was just one of the many things I loved about being with Dennis – our shared love of food and wine and the conversations that revolved around dining. I had never had that with anyone before.

However, the conversation wasn't really over. Driving home, Dennis turned to me and said, "Pauline, I don't want to let you go. I want to be here for you always. I care about you so much. I love Joanne and Ross as much as I love you and just so you know, I don't need children of my own. You, Joanne and Ross are all I need."

I listened and made no comment but quietly reflected on his words as we drove the rest of the way home. We kissed each other good night in the car. "Will I see you tomorrow?" I asked. "Of course you will. You know I can't resist seeing you," he said. I laughed and let myself out of the car. As I walked to the door, I could feel his eyes watching me until I was safely inside the restaurant.

That was another thing I loved about Dennis. *He always takes such good care of me and makes sure that I am always safe*, I thought as I walked up the stairs. I'd had two proposals this month – one for work and one for love. They each made me a little nervous and excited.

Poached Monkfish with Root Vegetables, Crispy Leeks, Chive Broth

It's all about the presentation of this poached monkfish with root vegetables and brussels sprouts topped with frizzled leeks.

Serves 6

Monkfish

3 pounds monkfish

3 cups water

6 carrots, peeled and cut into 3/4-inch slices

2 parsnips, peeled and cut into 3/4-inch slices

1 small rutabaga (swede), peeled and cut into 3/4-inch cubes

10 brussels sprouts, outer leaves removed

1 small bunch chives, chopped

4 tablespoons butter

kosher salt and white pepper

Cut the monkfish into 6 portions.

In a large saucepan, bring the water, salted, to a boil and add the carrots, parsnips, rutabaga, and brussels sprouts. Reduce the heat to a simmer and cook the vegetables for about 15 minutes, until fork tender. Remove the vegetables and measure out 2 cups of the vegetable water. Add the chopped chives and butter to the water.

Dry the monkfish and season to taste with salt and white pepper. Add the monkfish to the measured vegetable water and cook on medium-low heat for about 10 minutes. The fish is cooked when a knife inserted into the flesh comes out easily.

Crispy Leeks

1 leek, white part only, julienned *vegetable oil, for frying*

Parboil the julienned leek for barely 1 minute on medium-high heat. Strain in a sieve and place on paper towels to dry. Heat the vegetable oil in a saucepan on a medium-high heat, add the leeks, and cook for about 1 minute, until frizzled. Remove and drain on a paper towel.

To serve, cut the brussels sprouts into quarters. Place the vegetables in the center of a large shallow bowl. Top with the poached fish. Pour a ½ cup of the chive broth into the bowl and top with frizzled leeks.

Beef Carpaccio
with Mustard Caper Aioli

This dish arrived one evening in the middle of an awkward conversation. Even though I was unsure of my next words to Dennis, this elegant dish of very thin slices of seared beef tenderloin, served with a web of mustard caper aioli, required no words.

Serves 8

Beef Carpaccio

1 pound beef tenderloin
1 tablespoon of olive oil
sea salt and black pepper

You will also need:
plastic wrap

Heat a skillet over high heat. Season the tenderloin well with salt and pepper. Add the olive oil to the skillet and sear the tenderloin for about 10 minutes, until evenly browned on both sides but still rare in the middle. Remove and let cool, cover tightly with plastic wrap, and refrigerate for a minimum of 2 hours or until needed.

Mustard Caper Aioli

1 teaspoon of Dijon mustard
1 teaspoon of lemon juice
1 egg yolk
1 teaspoon of capers

½ cup of olive oil
salt and freshly ground black pepper
8 caper berries, for garnish

Place the mustard, lemon juice, egg yolk, and capers in a food processor and pulse to blend. Slowly drizzle in the olive oil until the mixture is the consistency of mayonnaise. Season to taste with salt and pepper and refrigerate until ready to serve.

To serve, slice the beef into paper-thin slices and cover each plate with one layer. Place the aioli in a piping bag and pipe a "web" around the beef. Garnish with caperberries in the center of the plate.

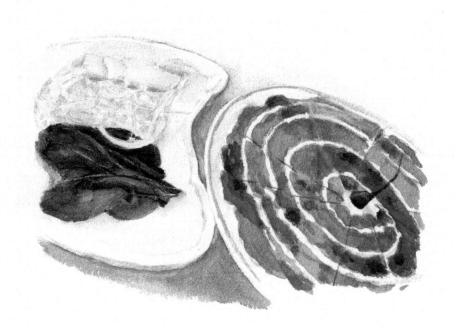

Salmon Parchment Parcels

This is very similar to the dish I had at Thornbury the night that Mr. Bell asked me to work there. It's a skinless salmon fillet enfolded in parchment paper (en papillote) with za'atar, lemon, butter, new potatoes, fava beans, and basil, served with a basil yogurt sauce.

Serves 4

Salmon Fillets

4 skinless 6-ounce salmon fillets
¼ cup extra virgin olive oil
½ cup dry white wine
2 garlic cloves, minced
juice of 1 lemon
1 tablespoon chopped fresh basil
1 teaspoon za'atar
16 small new potatoes, washed
  and halved

1 cup fresh or frozen fava beans
2 lemons, sliced
kosher salt and freshly ground
  black pepper

You will also need:
4 pieces 14 × 16 inch parchment paper

Preheat the oven to 400°F.

In a small bowl, combine the olive oil, white wine, garlic, the juice of 1 lemon, basil, za'atar, and a pinch of salt and pepper. Mix well. Cut the new potatoes in half and divide them between the parchment paper sheets with the fava beans. Place a salmon fillet on top and pour over the olive oil mixture. Top with lemon slices. Pull both sides of parchment paper to the center and seal all the way around. Place on a sheet pan. Transfer to the oven and bake for 20 minutes, or until the potatoes are tender.

Basil Yogurt Sauce

1 cup plain yogurt
juice of 1 lemon
1 pinch of crushed red pepper flakes

1 tablespoon finely chopped
    basil leaves
salt and white pepper

Place all the ingredients in a bowl and mix together well with a spatula.

Serve the salmon on a plate in its parchment parcel, with the sauce on the side.

Crème Brûlée

This was one of the most popular desserts at the castle. It's a rich, creamy baked vanilla bean custard topped with a crunchy toasted sugar crust.

Serves 6

1 quart heavy cream
1 vanilla bean, split and scraped
1 cup vanilla sugar*
6 large egg yolks

* sugar that has been infused with a vanilla bean

Preheat the oven to 325°F.

Place the cream with the vanilla bean and its pulp in a medium saucepan set over medium-high heat and stir until it comes to a boil. Remove from the heat, cover, and let stand for 15 minutes. Remove the vanilla bean.

In a medium bowl, whisk together half the sugar and the egg yolks until well blended and starting to lighten in color. Add the cream a little at a time, stirring continuously. Divide the mixture between six 8-ounce ramekins. Place the ramekins in a large sheet pan and pour enough hot water into the pan to come halfway up the sides of the ramekins. Bake for about 40–45 minutes, until the crème brûlée is set but still trembling in the center.

Remove the ramekins from the sheet pan and refrigerate for at least 2 hours and up to 3 days. Remove the crème brûlée from the refrigerator 30 minutes prior to browning the sugar on top. Divide the remaining sugar equally between the ramekins and spread evenly. Using a culinary torch, melt the sugar to form a crispy top (alternatively, place the ramekins under a broiler). Allow the crème brûlée to sit for at least 5 minutes before serving.

CHAPTER TEN

Falling in Love

It happened on one of those what we called "Sunday Kind of Love" days, after the song by Etta James. We loved the lyrics, because, as she sings, it was the kind of love that lasted past Saturday night. That just felt right to us.

To celebrate our Sunday kind of love, Dennis and I enjoyed one of our rituals by spending the day at Michael's, a comfy and sunny restaurant in Bristol along the River Avon. We spent many Sundays there, lunching leisurely with a bottle of fine wine and talking about life and putting the world to rights.

After lunch, we would settle by the fire in the lounge, reading the Sunday papers and sharing stories about what we had read. Quite often we would do the crossword puzzle together over a glass of port or champagne. The management never minded us lingering and we were often there for four or five hours before journeying home.

On this particular Sunday, we went with Alyson, the waitress from Blostin's, and Martin, her husband. We had known Alyson and Martin from when we first started dating. They were probably the only two people who had watched our love grow, besides Bill and Monica. They also lived just down the road from Blostin's and had two children, who were close in age to Joanne and Ross. We had told them about Michael's so many times that it was finally great to share it with them.

With our Bombay Sapphire gin and tonics in hand, we settled by a large window in the lounge that overlooked the river before ordering our food. The sun was streaming in and the river sparkled. It took us a while to determine our menu selections as we were talking and drinking. We were in no hurry!

When we got down to the business of ordering, I guided Alyson and Martin to some of my favorites, such as the Rosemary Garlic Bone-In Pork Chop finished with a splash of reduced white wine butter sauce and the Lamb Ragù Pappardelle Pasta. "Or, if you're in the mood for fish, the cod is crusted with coriander, paprika, and cumin, baked with lemon juice, olive oil, and lots of minced garlic with fresh cilantro and served with artichoke rice, also their carrot ginger soup is always good," I rattled on, suddenly realizing how deep my love of pairing people with just the right menu had become.

For myself I ordered the Spatchcocked Chicken Drenched with Garlic and Herbs and finished with a balsamic glaze. This was new to the menu and it was served with a Parmesan Sweet Pea Risotto, just perfect for the spring day. Lunch continued with more courses and conversation until we were full and then could rest back in our chairs, content, to finish the last sips of our wine.

At the end, as always, we indulged in a glass of port while Dennis told Alyson and Martin a story about something he'd experienced with Joanne and Ross that week. I was listening quietly to the conversation with my eyes focused on Dennis when suddenly the noise around me disappeared and all I could hear was Dennis's voice telling the story.

I'd heard of moments like this but had never experienced it. It was deathly silent, and I imagined I was suspended in a white space.

I felt the presence of magic, an angel, perhaps, who was sending me a message. At that very moment, I knew I loved Dennis. Was it something he was saying? I don't know, but I had a strong feeling of love and I knew I didn't want to lose him. I don't think he knew what I had just experienced as he still was deeply engaged with his tale. When he had finished speaking, he looked at me and smiled. I smiled back, knowing he was the one and that I loved him.

I realized that this sudden burst of love was a bit of bad timing on my part. Dennis had just decided to go to America to take on a once-in-a-lifetime opportunity to create a custom carpentry installation at an incredible property in Malibu. They were offering a work permit, accommodation, round trip airline tickets, and a handsome salary. Six months wasn't that long, I had told myself, and I had my position at Thornbury to keep me busy. But that afternoon at Michael's, all of a sudden six months felt like a lifetime.

I had myself to blame a bit. We had decided on this move together a few weeks earlier. It was a late night at Blostin's, before I had moved to the castle, when he unexpectedly came by. I was just closing up and while a couple sat at the last table in the house, nursing their glasses of wine, Dennis and I chatted quietly at the bar. "It will be for six months, Peeps," he said. "But it's a great opportunity." I agreed enthusiastically and said that six months was the last thing he should be thinking about right now.

Dennis understood the power of taking an opportunity when it came along. I knew he was hesitating because of me and I wanted him to make this decision free of that thought.

Dennis is one of six children. He'd left school at fifteen to enter a six-year journeyman apprenticeship. His first job after that was working for a company that built tract homes. Not very creative, but it was a good starting point, and he made a fair amount of money. When he was twenty-two, a chance meeting at a local pub with his friend Peter led to an opportunity for him to go on his own. Peter had started his own carpentry company and invited Dennis to join his team. Dennis gave up the security of his full-time job to work with Peter on custom homes. Eventually, Dennis went to work on his own project and on historic properties.

While picking up architectural fitments for it one day, Dennis and the supplier got chatting. "You're so busy every time I come by," Dennis said, curious about the business. "Is there really such a big market here for these specialty pieces?" The supplier replied that it wasn't England keeping him busy, but customers in America, and lately in California, who wanted this style. "California? Really?" Dennis said. Jokingly, he added, "If anyone there needs help installing these, give me a call!"

He left, thinking nothing of it until the supplier called a few weeks later. "I've got someone who needs some help in California, and I thought of you for the job. Do you want to meet him? He's in town this week."

Dennis went to meet John and they got on famously. John was a charismatic young entrepreneur from London who had bought property in Malibu. He had been living there with his family. He dreamed of building an English country estate with a windmill. Unfortunately, he wasn't able to find qualified tradesmen who understood how to put together the architectural pieces he had purchased in England. He had come back to find the right person to handle the project.

"This is a great opportunity," Dennis said again to me that night at Blostin's as we pored over all the pros and cons. He admitted there was an element of risk as he would have to let his clients know he would be gone and wrap up projects the best he could. "But then again," he countered, arguing the opposite side with himself, "the chance to work on a building like this from the ground up and to be able to use all my skills is just too attractive to turn down." But the downside was being apart for six months.

That night at Blostin's we went back and forth, considering everything. I was very supportive of the move as it did sound ideal. At the end of the evening, we both concluded that going there was the best thing for Dennis to do.

Not that it happened overnight. It took about five months to get all the paperwork in order. Those five months waiting became a roller coaster of uncertainties. On top of that I had to transition to Thornbury Castle. And on top of that, I had fallen in love. I don't know why, but I kept that to myself at the time. Maybe it was because he was going to America and I didn't want to hold him back. I can only guess now, looking back.

And so it was that a couple of months after our lunch at Michael's, Dennis had his ticket in hand for California and would leave on June 5, 1981.

A week before he was due to leave on this fabulous adventure, he called me spontaneously, asking me if I could join him for lunch at the King's Arms. "It's such a beautiful day," he said. And it was. We took the MG and opened the sunshine roof to let the sun pour into the car.

We were both in a carefree mood, enjoying our surroundings and making idle conversation as we drove to the pub. Everyone else must have had the same idea as us on this beautiful day, as the pub was crowded and busy. We eventually got ourselves a drink at the bar, ordering a simple ploughman's lunch as we squeezed into a table tucked into the corner of the room.

In some ways, it was the perfect spot. The sunlight through the partially curtained window fell in the center of our small, round, dark wood table. Our ploughman's lunch was served with a little twist – a warm Brie cheese wrapped in puff pastry. After a couple of bites trying to figure out what that delicious flavor was, I realized it was smothered with a sun-dried tomato pesto. It was at the beginning of this culinary trend and I wholeheartedly loved it.

After lunch, we ordered a glass of port before heading back.

As the waiter set our glasses down, we sighed almost at the same time, a bit melancholy upon realizing we were about to be apart for six months. "So, will you miss me when you're gone?" I leaned over the table to get closer to him.

"Without a doubt. I wish you were coming with me," he said.

"Me too, but one can't just pick up and go, especially with two children, uh?! Time will fly by," I continued, "and before you know it, it will be Christmas and you'll be back."

"Will you write to me?" he asked.

"Of course." By this time, we were close together, our elbows on the table, and we were holding hands.

He looked deeply into my eyes and said, "I am going to miss you so much, Peeps. I've never felt this way about anyone, and Joanne and Ross are so special to me. I love them and I love you." There was a pause, then: "Will you marry me?"

Without missing a beat, but with a knowing smile and a nod, I said, "I thought you would never ask. Yes, I'll marry you. I love you so very much." The kiss that followed was beautiful, just like the day. We got up and left, oblivious to all the people around us.

Neither of us knew that our lunch date was going to end up the way it did. None of this was planned, it just happened. We had committed our love to each other and now he was about to leave for America. We kept what had just happened to ourselves. A week later I was driving Dennis to London Heathrow airport.

We stayed at the Athenaeum Hotel in Mayfair the night before he left. We had now been dating for two and a half years and during this time our love had been consumed with wine, dining, and hospitality. We had discovered an extraordinary amount about food and wine, which had brought us even closer together. Who knew falling in love with Dennis would elevate my passion for food and wine to new heights?

Our interest in dining now took us to places we had never even thought about before. So it was that on his final night, we couldn't resist dining at Le Gavroche, one of the trendiest restaurants in London. It was owned by brothers Albert and Michel Roux and was the first restaurant in the UK to receive a two Michelin star rating. It served the very best of classic French food with the highest standards of cooking and service.

There was a strict dress code so Dennis wore his blazer, tie, and gray slacks, which made him even more handsome to me. I wore an emerald green and black floral print dress with a black wrap and black patent shoes and clutch. We were ready to indulge in one last extravagant meal together and were in a festive mood. We wanted to enjoy one another rather than feel the sadness of him leaving.

The evening proved to be romantic, less about the food and more about our love for each other. And yet the food highlights can't be ignored. We had an exquisite Cheese Soufflé, a fresh Salmon Tartare, and, not being able to resist lamb wherever I go, I had the Grilled Minted Mustard Lamb Chop with Spiced Eggplant. Dennis, I had learned, couldn't resist ordering scallops when they were on the menu. The dish that night was Scallops in a Sweet Pea Sauce with Gnocchi.

We were in love, something I think the whole restaurant and staff could see, although we didn't even notice. We only had eyes for each other as we drank our champagne and fabulous burgundy wine. A night to remember and an experience we will not forget.

We drove to Heathrow the next morning in silence. After going through security, I was able to wait with him at his gate until he boarded. We talked about something and nothing really, and then it was time for him to leave. We held each other in our arms for quite a while, we kissed, and then he picked up his carry-on, looked at me, and asked, "You will write to me, won't you?"

"Of course I will!"

With that, he turned and walked down the corridor to his plane, taking one last look back and blowing me a kiss.

I stood at the window watching his plane until it moved into position on the runway. I knew he couldn't see me, but it was important to me to stay there until the plane flew away. I looked a mess, with tears rolling down my cheeks, and I found myself waving as the plane took off. "Goodbye," I choked back quietly to myself.

I wiped my tears away the best I could before turning around, but they continued as I walked through the airport. I was sobbing all the way, keeping my head down so people could not see me crying. *Come on, Pauline, pull yourself together*, I thought. But they flowed for a little longer. It wasn't until I drove out of the parking lot that they subsided. I smiled to myself. *Oh my, I'm crying like a big baby, anyone would think I had been dreadfully hurt. So, this is what love and happiness feels like, uh?*

That night, I wrote my first letter to Dennis.

Mediterranean Spiced Baked Cod with Lemon Garlic Artichoke Rice

This is reminiscent of a dish Dennis and I enjoyed at one of the many bistros we ate at while dating. The spices and the lemon garlic artichoke rice made it memorable enough for me to continue making it at home.

Serves 4

Lemon Juice Mixture

5 tablespoons freshly squeezed lemon juice

5 tablespoons extra virgin olive oil
2 tablespoons melted butter

Combine the ingredients in a bowl and set aside.

Fish Spice Coating

⅓ cup all-purpose flour
1 teaspoon ground coriander
¾ teaspoon sweet Spanish paprika

¾ teaspoon ground cumin
¾ teaspoon sea salt
½ teaspoon black pepper

Combine the ingredients in a bowl and set aside.

Cod Fillets

1½ pounds cod fillets (4 pieces)
2 tablespoons olive oil

5 garlic cloves, peeled and minced finely
4 sprigs of rosemary, for garnish

Preheat the oven to 400°F.

Pat the cod fillets dry with paper towels. Dip the fillets in the lemon juice mixture then in the spice coating mixture. Shake off any excess coating. Reserve the remaining lemon juice mixture.

Heat the olive oil in a cast-iron skillet over medium-high heat. Add the cod fillets and sear on both sides to give color but do not fully cook. Remove from the heat and place on a sheet pan. Add the minced garlic to the reserved lemon juice mixture and drizzle over the cod fillets.

Bake in the oven for about 10 minutes, until the fish begins to flake easily with a fork. Serve immediately, garnished with a sprig of rosemary.

Lemon Garlic Artichoke Rice

1 tablespoon unsalted butter

2 cups chopped leeks, white part only

4 garlic cloves, chopped

2 cups canned quartered artichoke
 hearts

¾ cup dry white wine

2 cups chicken broth

zest of 1 large lemon

1 cup jasmine rice

sea salt and freshly ground
 black pepper

Melt the butter in a saucepan on medium heat. Add the leeks, garlic, and artichokes and season to taste with salt and pepper. Cook, stirring occasionally, for about 5 minutes, until the leeks are soft. Add the wine and cook, stirring, for about 5 minutes, until the liquid is reduced by half.

Add the broth, lemon zest, and rice and stir to combine. Reduce the heat to low. Cover and simmer for about 12 minutes, until fork tender. Remove from the heat and let stand, covered, for 10 minutes. Fluff with a fork and serve.

Rosemary Garlic Pork Chop
with White Wine Sauce

Pork chops are yet another meal I found as an important pathway to a man's heart. I love this version served with a dry white wine sauce sprinkled with coarse black peppercorns.

Serves 4

4 pork chops, bone in (1 inch thick)
olive oil, for brushing
1 yellow onion, chopped
8 rosemary sprigs
½ teaspoon chopped fresh thyme
1 cup dry white wine, such as
  sauvignon blanc
¾ cup low sodium chicken broth

1 teaspoon cornstarch
1 tablespoon cold water
1 teaspoon unsalted butter
coarse black peppercorns, for garnish
kosher salt and freshly ground
  black pepper

You will also need:
aluminum foil

Preheat the oven to 375°F.

Heat a cast-iron grill skillet over medium heat. Brush the pork chops with olive oil and sprinkle lightly with salt and pepper. Grill the chops on both sides until the grill marks are nice and brown, about 3 minutes on each side.

Remove the chops from the grill skillet and place on a half sheet pan. Add the chopped onion, 4 rosemary sprigs, chopped thyme, wine, and chicken broth. Cover with foil and bake in the oven for about 30 minutes, or until tender and the meat inside is a light pink.

Strain the cooking juices into a skillet over medium-high heat. Bring to a boil and reduce the juices slightly to concentrate the flavors. In a small cup, whisk the cornstarch with the water until smooth. Stir into the juices and continue cooking until slightly thickened. Whisk in the butter and stir until melted.

To serve, spoon the sauce over the pork chops and garnish each with a twist of coarse black peppercorns from a peppermill and a rosemary sprig.

Sun-Dried Tomato Brie en Croûte

When I first had this, sun-dried tomatoes were somewhat new, at least they were to me. The combination of the creamy warm Brie topped with sun-dried tomato pesto nestled in a golden puff pastry blanket is always one of my favorites.

Serves 6

1 whole (6-inch) triple crème
   Brie wheel
2 ounces sun-dried tomatoes from
   the jar
2 ounces powdered Parmesan cheese
2 tablespoons olive oil
1 teaspoon minced garlic

2 sheets store-bought puff pastry
1 egg
1 tablespoon milk
salt and freshly ground black pepper
toasted bread chunks, baguette,
   or crostini, to serve

Preheat the oven to 300°F.

Place the sun-dried tomatoes in a bowl, cover with boiling water, and let soak for 1 hour. Drain the tomatoes and remove the skins.

Place the tomatoes, Parmesan, olive oil, and garlic in a food processor and blend until smooth. Season to taste with salt and pepper.

Cut the rind off the top of the Brie and spread the sun-dried tomato pesto over the cut surface. Roll out one sheet of puff pastry. Place it over the Brie and wrap it round, sealing it underneath.

Whisk the egg and milk together. Cut small pastry hearts or leaves from the remaining sheet of pastry and place them around the top of the Brie. Brush the top and sides of the pastry with the egg wash.

Bake in the oven for about 45 minutes, until the pastry is golden and the cheese has melted inside.

Cut a circle in the top and remove the pastry. Stir the sun-dried tomato pesto into the melted cheese. Serve with toasted bread chunks, baguette, or crostini.

Cheese Soufflé

Everyone should have a cheese soufflé in their repertoire. It's the perfect dish for an elegant night at home, or a Sunday night movie date. This warm fluffy cheese soufflé, made with Parmigiano and Gruyère cheese and garnished with micro greens, is perfection.

Serves 4

¼ cup plus 2 tablespoons freshly
  grated Parmigiano Reggiano cheese
3 tablespoons unsalted butter
3 tablespoons all-purpose flour
1¼ cups heavy cream
4 large eggs, separated, plus 3 large
  egg whites
3 tablespoons dry sherry

1½ cups shredded Gruyère cheese
2 tablespoons sour cream
1¼ teaspoons kosher salt
1 teaspoon Dijon mustard
½ teaspoon dry mustard
¼ teaspoon cayenne pepper
¼ teaspoon cream of tartar
micro greens, for garnish

Preheat the oven to 375°F.

Butter a 1½ quart soufflé dish (or 4 individual ramekins) and coat it (them) with the 2 tablespoons of Parmigiano.

In a medium saucepan, melt the butter. Stir in the flour to make a paste. Gradually whisk in the cream and bring to a boil over moderate heat, whisking. Reduce the heat to low and cook, whisking, for 3 minutes, until very thick. Transfer to a large bowl and let cool. Stir in the egg yolks, sherry, Gruyère, sour cream, salt, Dijon mustard, dry mustard, cayenne, and the ¼ cup of Parmigiano.

Put the 7 egg whites in a large stainless-steel bowl and add the cream of tartar. Using an electric mixer, beat the whites until firm peaks form. Fold one-third of the whites into the soufflé base to lighten it, then fold in the remaining whites until no streaks remain.

Scrape the mixture into the prepared soufflé dish. Run your thumb around the inside rim of the dish to remove any crumbs. Bake for 35 minutes, or until the soufflé is golden brown and puffed. Serve immediately, garnished with micro greens.

Scallops in Sweet Pea Sauce with Gnocchi

During our time exploring restaurants together, I learned that Dennis simply can't resist scallops if they are on the menu. This dish is based on the one we enjoyed at Le Gavroche in London before he left for six months in America.

Serves 4

Gnocchi

2 potatoes, peeled and cut into 6 pieces
2 cups all-purpose flour

1 egg
1 tablespoon olive oil

Bring a large pot of salted water to a boil, add the potatoes, and cook for about 15 minutes, until tender but still firm. Drain the potatoes, let cool, and mash with a fork or potato masher.

In a large bowl, combine 1 cup of the mashed potatoes with the flour and egg. Knead until the dough forms a ball. Shape small portions of the dough into long snakes and cut each snake into 1-inch pieces.

Bring a large pot of lightly salted water to a boil. Drop in the gnocchi and cook for 3–5 minutes or until the gnocchi rise to the surface. Drain the gnocchi on a plate lined with a paper towel.

Heat a medium skillet on a medium-low heat and add the olive oil. Add gnocchi to the pan, being sure not to crowd the pieces, and sear until golden in color. Remove from the pan to a plate lined with a paper towel.

Sweet Pea Sauce

1½ cups fresh sweet peas, blanched,
  plus extra for garnish
¾ cups chicken stock
3 tablespoons heavy cream

¼ teaspoon kosher salt
⅛ teaspoon freshly ground black
  pepper

Place the peas, chicken stock, cream, salt, and pepper in a blender and blend until smooth. When ready to serve, place the mixture in a small saucepan and warm for 2 minutes over very low heat.

Scallops

12 large dry scallops
3 tablespoons canola oil
2 tablespoons unsalted butter

1 lemon
kosher salt
chopped flat-leaf parsley, for garnish

Season the scallops generously on both sides with salt, then place on a plate lined with a paper towel and let sit for 15 minutes. Gently pat the scallops dry, then season again lightly on one side with salt.

Over high heat, heat a skillet large enough to fit all the scallops so they are not touching. When the skillet is hot, add the canola oil. Carefully place the scallops in the pan and cook for about 1 minute on each side until golden brown. Add the butter to the pan, flip the scallops, and cook for a further minute on one side. Transfer the scallops to a plate and squeeze with fresh lemon juice.

For each serving, spoon warm sweet pea sauce around the base of a shallow bowl. Arrange the scallops in the center and surround them with crispy gnocchi. Sprinkle with some whole peas and chopped flat-leaf parsley.

CHAPTER ELEVEN

Love Letters

I arrived home at the castle from saying goodbye to Dennis at the airport, feeling quite exhausted. I slowly walked up the gray flagstone steps into our living quarters with suitcase in hand and fell into the big green armchair, my arms flopped over the sides. I put my head back on the pillow, closed my eyes for a moment, and sighed deeply.

We had now been living at the castle for a couple of months. Mr. Bell had renovated the gatehouse into living quarters for me, Joanne and Ross. Our new home was indeed special. I knew that not many people got to work in a sixteenth-century castle and live in its gatehouse. Our rooms were like the rest of the castle – constructed from thick stone walls with arched windows with black iron dividers and iron handles. Each window had a deep recess that became a shelf for a few flowering plants. The ceilings were lined with dark wooden beams. I had brought my furniture from Blostin's, which, while not in keeping with the castle, looked like home. It was all very comfortable, and perfect for our needs.

The children were still at Angela's. I didn't have to pick them up until after school the next day, which gave me time to get unpacked and enjoy a quiet night to myself with my thoughts.

I picked up the phone to let Angela know I was home. "How did it go?" she asked.

"Great. The hotel and dinner were fabulous, the plane was on time, and I was sad to see him go. Dennis was a little nervous as he has no idea what he's getting into, but he's ready for the adventure," I said, giving her a brief rundown.

Thankfully, Angela had given up asking about the status of our relationship and whether we were ever going to get married. And yet the family had hoped we might announce an engagement before he left. But that didn't happen and now that we were spending six months apart, I was sure they wondered if it ever would.

"How have the children been?" I asked.

"Just fine," she said. "The four of them play well together, which is just as well since they go to the same school. I think it's made it easier on them going from one school to another, don't you think?" she mused.

"Absolutely," I replied. Once again, I was grateful that Joanne and Ross had taken everything so easily in their stride, especially because the move from Blostin's to the castle was not the easiest of transitions either emotionally or logistically.

We had to put all our belongings in storage and live with Angela and Graham for a month because the accommodations at the castle weren't ready. Eva, their daughter, was the same age as Joanne. They were very close yet always generous with Ross, who would hang out and play with them. Their son, Ryan, was a little younger, but that didn't seem to matter. They had a full house. We were a disruption, but we worked it all out.

Dennis helped me with the move and was a pillar of strength when it came to physically getting things into storage. Unfortunately, this meant that we were moving twice in the space of a month – not a chore I embraced, but I had no choice. We had set a time when I would leave Blostin's and a time when I would begin working at the castle and it had to work.

Emotionally, leaving Blostin's was harder than I thought it would be. It was just as well we didn't drag out the farewell with a big fanfare. Bill was moving back into the apartment above the restaurant by himself while he and Monica sorted out the details of their divorce. They had found a buyer for the restaurant, but it seemed the sale was taking its time. Uncertainty was the norm.

As I hung up the phone to Angela, it struck me – I was alone in the gatehouse for the first time. It was so quiet. I got dressed for bed and opened a bottle of Crozes Hermitage. There was a bag of potato chips in the pantry. *That would do perfectly*, I thought, as I turned on the music, sat back with my feet on the ottoman, and looked back at those last days at Blostin's.

On the very last day I wandered around the apartment with key in hand, checking to be sure I hadn't forgotten anything. Dennis had already left with the moving truck and Joanne and Ross were with my sister. I glanced around our apartment above the restaurant and couldn't help but reflect on what had happened these last few years. So many changes, all good. It made me smile, as it held nothing but fond memories.

As I walked down the stairs for the last time, Bill was there standing at the bottom, looking up. "Well, Miss Pauline, time to go, uh?" he said with his usual half-smile.

I wasn't expecting him to be there and suddenly I felt a little choked. "Bill, I thought we said our goodbyes last night," I said. "You're torturing me." And we gave each other a big hug.

"I will never forget you, Monica, and Blostin's for giving me this opportunity, Bill. Thank you. You've changed my life forever and to think when you invited me to work at the restaurant I said, 'But, what would I do here?'" We both laughed at the memory and how ridiculous those words now sounded.

"Go get 'em," Bill said, pushing me away – and, I could tell, brushing away a tear. "You are going to conquer the world. And make sure you take care of my man, Dennis. Now go before you make me cry." With that, I dropped the key in his hands and walked swiftly out the door, which Bill closed immediately behind me.

Getting in the car, I took one more glance at the restaurant. *This was an amazing chapter in my life I will never forget*, I thought to myself as I drove away. *Oh my, and here I am branching out again in new unknown territories working in a castle, and on top of that I'm in love with a man who's just left me for six months*. I had to laugh.

That night, nestled in with my wine and chips, I began my first love letter to Dennis while he was still flying toward America. As I started writing, emotions I had never felt before began to pour out. The words flowed. *To think that I wondered what I'd write about*, I thought, as I finished the last line in a seven-page letter. I sealed the envelope with a kiss and a smile.

I had to find his address (it would soon be committed to memory) and as I addressed the letter I wondered if he'd landed safely. What time was it there now? I snuggled between the cold bed sheets with a shudder and drifted into a light sleep.

The next day, before picking up the children, I went to the post office to weigh my letter and get enough stamps for the month. I popped it in the red post box and was hopeful he would get it within four or five days.

This was the beginning of a ritual, as every single day over the next six months, however late, I went to bed with my glass of red wine and would share my day, thoughts, and love for him in a letter. Dennis did the same. Some days I would have two letters, as we had two post deliveries in the day then. The postman got to know me. Since we were in a castle, there was no post box. He used to knock on the castle's kitchen door to give us our letters. Or, if we were out on the grounds, I'd meet him there. I don't believe he'd actually met

Dennis, but he always asked about him. It cheered him up when I told him that Dennis was getting on fine.

As for myself and the children, we got used to the routine of living at the castle. They loved it. There was so much space to run around, and we had some farm animals that they enjoyed as well. Often, they would go to the main kitchen and have breakfast at the counter, sitting on stools. It made them feel quite grown-up to be in the main area of the castle, which normally was off limits to them.

The castle's manager was Fernando. He was originally from Spain and he and his wife, Lola, had lived at the castle for five years by the time we arrived. They had two children the same ages as Ross and Joanne. All of them built quite a bond and would play together. It was all perfect and once again, Joanne and Ross seemed to have adjusted to another move in life.

It was a little different for me, or at least this move was. The move itself was horrendous and my fear was off the charts, but Dennis was always ready with a supportive word.

Quite often I felt a little overwhelmed by the work. It was a different level of food, wine, and service, and the clientele had much higher expectations than those who frequented Blostin's. And whereas Bill and Monica were kind, warm, and accepting, Mr. Bell was a different beast. I had so much more to learn about fine dining and wine, and I sometimes felt it was way over my head. Mr. Bell was not that tolerant of mistakes. He didn't suffer fools gladly, so I always had to be ready to go above and beyond. He kept me on my toes and sometimes I would feel sorry for myself and shed a tear or two.

I found out from his assistant that he was disappointed in my performance. That shook my confidence. What did it mean? Somehow he had expected so much more from me as a leader. He wanted me to take charge and be stronger with regards to opening the hotel. It was harsh and I found myself really daunted by what was expected of me. I thought I was doing alright but obviously just doing the job wasn't enough.

I made sure not to let it slide. I wanted to learn and that means sometimes having hard conversations. So I asked him to tell me about my failings and how I could elevate my position to make an impact on opening the hotel as well as running the restaurant. I asked for a second chance.

It was an important lesson to learn. Here I was, thinking I was the bee's knees, but really, for the first time ever, my boss was disappointed in my performance.

From that point on, I took the bull by the horns and started doing my job with authority. I reported my progress regularly to him. We talked a lot about the challenges and the solutions until he could see that I had it under control. This was a job and a half, and every ounce of my body was focused on what I was doing at all times. This, together with taking care of the children, meant I was working 24/7, if not physically then in my mind. The only light relief was writing letters to Dennis, who obviously got the brunt of all the good, bad, and ugly!

I was a quick learner and with the help of Pepe, who had been working there as a waiter for eight years, and of course Fernando, I received tremendous guidance. At first they had frowned on Mr. Bell's choice of a new girl who only had bistro-level hospitality skills. I had to work hard to prove myself. Fernando in particular was skeptical of a woman, but he warmed to me and we found ourselves eventually enjoying working together.

These two friends were instrumental for my success in doing the job. I was starting to see the light and was picking up the art of hospitality as well as learning more and more about the food, wine, and service than I ever thought possible.

At one point, just as I felt I was turning a corner, Mr. Bell asked me to join him to dine with some important guests from other restaurant hotels. This scared me to death. Normally his girl-friend, Molly, accompanied him for these business dinners, but she was abroad at the time.

"Pauline," Mr. Bell prepped me, "there will be a lot of conversation about how these people turned their restaurants into a hotel. They are all Relais & Châteaux properties, and I think it would be advantageous to listen and learn and ask any questions that might be beneficial for us to know. After all, you will be running the show and the more you know, the better for us all." Nothing like being thrown in the deep end. But it was nice that he had faith in me. I took deep breaths and kept going.

Dinner that evening was, as always, served French style. This style was new to me when I joined the castle. Guests were presented with serving platters from the left. After they acknowledged the meal, the waiter would place it on their dinner plate. The service style was an art form, and in my spare time I practiced picking up peas with the fork and spoon. It wasn't easy, but as time went on, I perfected the skill.

This evening, Mr. Bell had chosen the same menu for all the guests. The meal began with a beautiful Coquilles St. Jacques, made with bay scallops and poached shrimp. This was followed by a Chicken Piccata, served in a lemony butter garlic sauce with capers. The vegetables – Butter Poached Haricots Verts and a Hasselback Potato with fresh thyme from our herb garden – were served on a side plate.

The evening conversation was all new territory to me. I had never been part of opening a hotel. All the owners, including Mr. Bell, were very entrepreneurial in spirit and opened their restaurants and hotels without any formal training, although most of them were trained chefs. They all had a passion for food, wine, and hospitality and found ways to make a living by converting their manor homes and castles into restaurants. And, with the help of architects and designers, turning their restaurants into hotels. They were all leaders in the restaurant world and well respected in this field of business, so the transition to being a hotel was a natural one.

That is exactly how we expanded the castle into a seven-room hotel. We researched various systems, trained ourselves on how they worked, and even did some on-site training in neighboring guest restaurants and hotels. We learned as we went. As we would tell one another – we are in hospitality. It's not rocket science. Quite simply, what that meant was giving guests a positive, helpful, personalized, friendly, quality experience, with plenty of attention to detail.

Things were going well, and yet when I was alone my insecurities would pop up. At least I was in my own country, surrounded by family and friends to talk to. Dennis was in an unknown land by himself, facing a new culture. He had so many things to overcome. His surroundings could not have been more different from mine. While I was in a castle, he was living in a small trailer on a property in Malibu, not luxurious by any means. The owners, John and Hannah, also lived on the property with their three children, in a three-bedroom trailer.

The family was very kind to Dennis and invited him over for dinner or took him out to dinner, knowing he was by himself. In our letters, I learned about the food he was discovering – Mexican cuisine, sushi, burgers, and deli foods – all things neither of us had eaten in England. But just as he had been in England with me, he was always open to new food experiences.

Even with the kindness of John and Hannah, and all the new adventures he was having, my letters were a comfort to him. He was lonely and missed us all dreadfully. The job was slow to start, waiting on permits and inclement weather. But he kept himself busy by building the architectural pieces for the house and working on the window frames, which he was building by hand. He was quite a novelty to the other workers, who were surprised he was building all the fitments with no electrical machinery, just hand tools.

In addition to our daily love letters, we also had a weekly phone call on Sundays. One Sunday, while I was having dinner with my parents, the phone rang. I answered it. I was slouching on the phone stool with my back against the wall, when suddenly I sat up straight. "Do I what?" I asked incredulously. My mum looked up at me, mouthing the words, "Is everything OK?" On the other end of the line, Dennis repeated the question. "What do you think about coming here and starting our lives together in California?"

Coquilles St. Jacques

This luxurious dish was popular at the castle. It's a preparation of scallops and shrimp in a creamy sauce under a crust of breadcrumbs and Gruyère cheese.

Serves 6

8 tablespoons unsalted butter

¼ cup all-purpose flour

1½ cups seafood stock

1 cup heavy cream

¼ teaspoon curry powder

1 cup large shallots, peeled and diced

12 ounces cremini mushrooms,
  stems discarded, sliced

¼ cup brandy

1½ cups of fresh breadcrumbs
  (about 6 crustless slices)

5 ounces shredded Gruyère cheese

¼ cup minced parsley

¼ cup extra virgin olive oil

1 pound bay scallops

1 pound shrimp, cut in small pieces

sea salt and freshly ground
  black pepper

3 lemons, halved and grilled,
  to serve

Preheat the oven to 400°F.

Melt half the butter in a saucepan over medium heat. When it foams, add the flour and cook for 4 minutes, whisking constantly. Add the stock and whisk again, until the mixture is smooth and thick. Add the cream and curry powder and season to taste with salt and pepper. Bring the sauce to a boil, lower the heat, and simmer for about 10 minutes, stirring occasionally, until it thickens. Set aside.

Melt 3 tablespoons of the butter in a large sauté pan over medium heat. When it foams, add the shallots and cook until they are clear and tender. Add the sliced mushroom caps and cook for

8–10 minutes until they have released their liquid and are just starting to brown. Stir in the brandy and cook for 1–2 minutes, until the alcohol has mostly evaporated. Season to taste with salt and pepper. Add the mushroom mixture to the cream sauce and set aside.

Combine the breadcrumbs, Gruyère, and parsley in a large bowl, then stir in the olive oil.

With the remaining tablespoon of butter, grease 6 scallop shell dishes. Divide the scallops and shrimp between the dishes and top with the cream and mushroom sauce. Top each dish with a handful of the breadcrumb mixture. Place the dishes on a sheet tray.

Cook for about 20 minutes or until the topping is lightly browned and bubbling and the scallops and shrimp are cooked through. Serve with a grilled lemon half to squeeze over the dish.

Chicken Piccata with Hasselback Potatoes and Haricots Verts

This is one of those pleasing dishes that is in almost every restaurant's repertoire. Thin medallions of chicken breast are cooked with garlic, white wine, and capers. At the castle, we served them with new season hasselback potatoes and a bundle of haricots verts.

Serves 4

Hasselback Potatoes

8 medium russet potatoes, scrubbed
8 tablespoons softened butter
½ cup extra virgin olive oil

⅓ cup finely chopped chives
kosher salt and freshly ground pepper

Preheat the oven to 450°F.

In a small bowl, combine the butter, olive oil, and chives and season to taste with salt and pepper.

Place a potato lengthwise between the handles of two wooden spoons. Slice the potato widthwise into thin slices, leaving ¼ inch at the bottom unsliced. The spoon handles will prevent you from slicing the potato all the way through. Repeat with the remaining potatoes.

Place the potatoes on a baking sheet tray and brush on the butter mixture, making sure to get in between all the slices. Bake for 55–60 minutes, until crisp on the outside and tender inside.

Chicken Piccata

2 skinless and boneless chicken
   breasts, butterflied, cut in half,
   and lightly pounded
all-purpose flour, for dredging
4 tablespoons unsalted butter
3 tablespoons extra virgin olive oil
½ cup of chicken stock

⅓ cup fresh lemon juice
¼ cup of brined capers, rinsed
chopped fresh flat-leaf parsley,
   for garnish
sea salt and freshly ground
   black pepper

Season the chicken to taste with salt and pepper then dredge in the flour, shaking off the excess.

In a large skillet over medium-high heat, melt the butter and olive oil. When the fat begins to sizzle, add the chicken and cook for 3 minutes on each side. Add the chicken stock, lemon juice, and capers and simmer for about 2 minutes, until cooked through.

Transfer the chicken to dinner plates, pour the sauce liberally over the chicken, and garnish with chopped parsley.

Haricots Verts Bundles

6 long chives
36 haricots verts

½ stick butter, melted
kosher salt and cracked black pepper

Place the chives in a small bowl, cover with boiling water to soften, then drain.

Trim the tops only of the beans. Divide the beans into 6 bundles and tie each bundle in the middle with a chive. Place the bundles in a steamer over a saucepan half filled with simmering water. Cover the steamer and steam the beans over medium heat for 5–8 minutes, or until just tender.

Drizzle the bean bundles with the melted butter and sprinkle with salt and cracked black pepper.

Lemon Syllabub with a Chocolate Macaron

This elegant dessert served at the castle begins with cream whipped with sweet white wine and lemon zest and juice, served in a glass topped with a curl of lemon peel, chocolate shavings, and a chocolate macaron.

Serves 4

Lemon Syllabub

1 cup heavy whipping cream
½ cup white sugar
¼ cup sweet white wine
⅛ cup freshly squeezed lemon juice
1 teaspoon grated lemon zest

For garnish:
4 curls of lemon peel
chocolate shavings

Whip the cream and sugar in a chilled bowl until the cream begins to thicken. Gradually whip in the white wine, lemon juice, and lemon zest. Continue to whip until light and fluffy but not grainy.

Serve in chilled 6-ounce glasses, topped with a curl of lemon peel and chocolate shavings.

Chocolate Macarons

1 cup almond flour

¾ cup powdered sugar

2 tablespoons cocoa powder

3 large egg whites, room temperature

½ cup granulated sugar

Line two baking sheets with parchment paper or silicone baking mats. Trace 8 1½-inch circles, spacing them a couple of inches apart.

Sift the almond flour, powdered sugar, and cocoa powder through a fine mesh sieve. Sift a second time to make sure the ingredients are thoroughly mixed and light. Set aside.

In a mixer, whisk the egg whites on medium speed for about 1 minute, until foamy. Gradually add the granulated sugar, 1 tablespoon at a time. Once all the sugar is added, continue to beat until stiff peaks form. Add the sifted almond flour mixture to the stiff egg whites and fold them in by mixing with a spatula from the bottom of the bowl, lifting it up to drop onto the top of the mixture.

Preheat the oven to 300°F.

Transfer the macaron batter to a pastry bag fitted with a large round piping tip. Pipe the batter into the circles on the parchment paper or silicone mat.

Bake for about 16–18 minutes until they are crispy. Let the shells cool completely before removing them from the parchment paper or silicone mat and before piping the ganache filling, recipe overleaf.

Ganache filling

⅔ cup semisweet chocolate chips   *⅓ cup heavy cream*

Melt the chocolate chips and cream in a medium saucepan over low heat. Place in the refrigerator and let cool completely. Once cooled, place in a piping bag with a small nozzle and pipe onto the bottom side of half the macaron shells. Match up with the top shells to finish.

CHAPTER TWELVE
A Trip to California

Heathrow Airport was madness. There had been another airline strike and it seemed there were thousands of people everywhere. Bodies were laid out on the floor and people were sleeping with their heads on their hand luggage. It seemed I might be joining them soon. My flight to Los Angeles had been canceled and I was stranded.

Well, this isn't a great beginning, I thought. When Dennis called me at my parents' and asked me what I thought of starting our lives together in California, he could hear the hesitation in my voice. There were so many things to consider – I had just started a new position and I was proud to say I was having some success in getting established at Thornbury Castle. The divorce was now final and the children had settled wonderfully into our new situation. If I were to move to California, I'd have to get sole custody and I wasn't sure my ex-husband would be too happy about that. At the very least, I knew he would put up a fight so the children couldn't leave the country. And what about green cards?

"That's not a problem, Peeps," Dennis said when I brought that up. "John said he could get them for all of us." That was good to hear. But still... "Why don't you come over and take a look for yourself as to what it is like and we can talk about the possibilities," Dennis continued. That sounded reasonable – after all, I should at least see what it was all about. Yes, I could make that happen – the children were going to be on summer break soon, which meant David would have them for two weeks. "OK, let me ask Mr. Bell if I can take some time off. And if I can get a vacation visa then I'll come over, how does that sound?"

"It sounds like we have a plan." I heard Dennis chuckle on the other end of the line. "I'll get you a round trip ticket once you give me the dates. Let's not talk about the thoughts of possibly living here before we've decided what would be best for us," he said.

"I agree, I'm just coming for a vacation to see what your life is all about in California," I said.

So here I was on my vacation, which was looking less and less like it was going to happen. One last time, I approached the air hostess to get an update. Instead of the usual answer, she chirped happily, "Do you want to fly to San Francisco? I have one seat left. It leaves in an hour." I was floored. Yes, yes, I said, not even knowing how far San Francisco was from Los Angeles, but at least it was in California. I hoped Dennis could pick me up.

I waded through all the bodies toward the airport pay phone. I had to tell Dennis of the change in plans. Damn, I got an answering machine. I left a detailed message and hoped he would get it in time to meet me in San Francisco. I boarded the plane, not knowing whether he would be there when I landed or not.

On the plane, the magazine in the seat pocket in front of me had some great articles, but it also had a map at the back. I looked up California and my heart sank. Oh my gosh, San Francisco is about three hundred miles from Malibu. That's about the length of England! *Well*, I thought, just before shutting my eyes to get some sleep, *there's no going back now.*

In San Francisco, I got through customs with no problem. I was tired. My suitcase felt heavy, and I looked bedraggled. As I made my way through a sea of exhausted people, I turned the corner toward the exit sign taking me out to arrivals. I scanned the faces of people waiting for their loved ones, and there he was. Dennis! We spotted each other at the same time and before I knew it, he was jumping over the ropes and running toward me. I dropped my suitcase as he gathered me in his arms and lifted me off the ground for a big hug and kiss. It was just like all those movies I loved and I laughed to myself, giddy that he was there.

He picked up my suitcase, and with my arm around his waist, we walked to the parking lot. We had so much to say but all we could do was kiss each other.

"I can't believe you made it here! I saw how far it was and—"

He stopped me with a kiss, then quickly told me that as soon as he heard my message, he jumped in the car. "I didn't know where San Francisco was either!" he said, laughing. Of course, he was also new to California. "John told me what freeways to take, and I drove as fast as I could. I'm amazed I made it." We just laughed at the absurdity of it all and shook our heads, glad it had worked out.

Dennis had driven for almost eight hours to meet my plane. There was no way we'd make it back to Los Angeles and the reservation he had made earlier at the Hotel Bel-Air. Instead, we stayed at the Hilton San Francisco Airport Hotel, which, from what I understood, was not the same thing at all! But did I care? We were together and had two whole weeks ahead of us. And we were in San Francisco, about to discover California together. This was new to him as well, because for the last couple of months he had really gone no further afield than Malibu and parts of Los Angeles.

That night, we both slept well after our long day of traveling to each other from different parts of the world. We woke up happy and hungry. Over breakfast, with a Thomas Guide and a map of California in hand, we began planning our route, but not before I fully took in what breakfast in America meant.

It was my first meal there and I was staggered by it. First, a restaurant hostess showed us to our table and gave us menus. This would never happen in England. We always just found our own tables. We were instantly served iced water and asked if we wanted tea or coffee, which appeared immediately. All this happened before the server came to the table, which was good as we needed the time to look at the menu. I was overwhelmed. I had never seen a menu that big.

"What can I get for you today?" our waitress asked. She was dressed in a black-and-white uniform and was poised with a pen and small pad in hand. I had given up on the menu and decided to just ask for what I wanted. "I would simply like eggs with bacon, sausage, and toast, and by chance would they have any baked beans?" I asked.

"Sorry, we don't have baked beans. How would you like your eggs?" I looked at Dennis as if to say, *How do I like my eggs?* We have no choice in England. They simply come cooked. Dennis answered for me. "She'll have them over easy." "Would you like rye, whole wheat or sourdough toast?" the waitress continued. I fumbled before choosing whole wheat. Toast was always just white bread in England. What's more, they kept refilling the water and my coffee. Dennis told me you can have as many refills as you like at no extra charge. Again, in England, you were charged by the cup.

"You should have warned me how it worked, Dennis. I feel a bit silly."

He just laughed. He'd been through it and knew what a shock an American breakfast was to a Brit. "Now, why would I do that and spoil the fun of you ordering your own first breakfast in California? It's something else, isn't it?"

"It certainly is," I said quietly, in awe. If this was breakfast, what would dinner be like?

Our journey began in San Francisco. Dennis was now used to driving "on the wrong side of the road" and was doing a great job navigating all the lanes and looking for the direction signs. "This is the big city, uh?" I said as I closed my eyes, nervous of how close we came to hitting something. Neither of us had ever seen traffic like this. There were six lanes on either side of the road. We were used to one each way or, at the most, a double-laned road. Coming from the English countryside, San Francisco was daunting.

We soon discovered navigation was not my strong point. I was useless knowing north from south and got us lost on many occasions. Thank goodness we were not in any hurry. It was all part of the experience, I told myself.

I was pleasantly surprised to find out how influential Mr. Bell was in Northern California and how ahead of his time he was as a restaurateur. Back in England, he had amassed an impressive wine cellar filled with predominantly French and German wines that he was always excited to share with his clientele. But he was also one of the first to explore the wines of America, specifically Napa, which was just starting to gain its worldwide reputation.

At the time, when Paul Masson carafe wine was the American wine most widely known in England, Mr. Bell was serving Trefethen, Mondavi, and Firestone wines as house wines. Usually the term "house wine" refers to something cheap and cheerful, an inexpensive choice for most diners. To Mr. Bell, though, a "house wine" was truly that – his special wine of the house on a given night. He enjoyed introducing his guests to new wines and he was always bold in his selections. He was also careful to give his wait-staff and management team an education in wine. I was honored to work with an owner who was so passionate about food and wine, who wanted to share his knowledge. It was such an exceptional education for me, and it continued during this trip.

Knowing I was going on vacation to California, Mr. Bell very graciously reached out by telex (no fax machines yet) to the Mondavi, Trefethen, and Firestone wineries, as well as a few restaurateurs, so we could visit and introduce ourselves.

That first night in San Francisco, we took advantage of his resources, dining out at a place called Monroe. At the mention of Mr. Bell, we were welcomed with open arms and treated like VIPs. The owner took care of us personally and assigned a personal waiter. "If it's OK," he said, "I'd like to serve you some of our specialty dishes. Is there anything you don't like?"

"We love everything," was our response.

"Then, please sit back and enjoy."

That we did! We sat back and soon became overwhelmed with all the food that came our way. We began with Deviled Eggs topped with Caviar. Neither of us had eaten a deviled egg, much less one finished with caviar. They were rich and creamy and unforgettable. Next, we were served asparagus with a light lemony hollandaise sauce, then a single large Ricotta Ravioli laced with a Tomato Beurre Blanc and finished with a crispy basil leaf. "Amazing," we murmured between bites.

A John Dory Fish Fillet was pan-fried and served with a drizzle of lemon butter sauce on a bed of wilted spinach. Next to it was half a lemon covered with a yellow net to catch any seeds when it was squeezed over the fish. I made a note to bring this back to the restaurant. Our patrons would love it. As we continued to indulge in the food, the owner brought us wine that paired with what he was serving, all from the Napa and Sonoma regions.

Just as we thought the marathon dinner was over, the waiter brought a Medallion of Venison in a light red wine sauce served with a dollop of Sweet Potato Herb Mash. The meal finally came to an end with a citrus sorbet served in a small champagne coupe.

We finally looked up from our meal, holding our stomachs as we sat back. For the first time, I noticed our booth. It was leather studded and had a small chandelier floating above. I also noticed that the restaurant was full. We hadn't noticed that it had been filling up, as our attention had been completely captivated by the food and wine – or was it by each other? *Both*, I thought.

When the owner came over and served our dessert, a cheese-cake with strawberry sauce, I looked at him and said, "I am certain we cannot eat another bite." And with that, I put my fork into the cake and took a bite.

He watched me as I did so, happy with my reaction. It was perfectly creamy yet thick enough to linger on the roof of my mouth. My eyes and smile told him how incredible I thought it was. He smiled, very pleased that he had two extremely satisfied customers.

"Please tell Kenneth hello and let him know he is always welcome here." And with that he was gone, leaving us to enjoy espresso and petits fours. We waited for a bill to arrive, but none came, an example of the generosity that exists in the culinary world as well as testimony to the stellar reputation of Mr. Bell. We felt extremely lucky that we were now part of his world.

The next day we were up and ready to go to the Napa Valley, with the hopes of visiting the Trefethen and Mondavi wineries. Believe it or not, we had never been to a winery, so this again was to be a new experience. I say we had never been to a winery and yet Thornbury Castle had its own tiny vineyard, as did Pilton, where Dennis was born. But both were private vineyards –the castle wine was for consumption in the restaurant, while Pilton wine was only sold locally. In all honesty, neither wine was that pleasant, although these were early days for modern English viticulture.

But this was different. America was so vast as we drove through Napa, so different from England. But it had its charms, such as the impressive stone buildings so prolific in Napa. Many were built to mimic French and English architecture. Others were more Californian in flavor, such as Trefethen, an earth-toned building at the end of a very long driveway. It blended with the vineyards and the landscaping and looked quite charming. However, we missed seeing it closer as no one was there.

Our next stop was Mondavi Winery, which had also been built to pay homage to the region's beginnings. The building was another architectural icon, designed in the style of California's missions with an expansive entryway arch and bell tower. We had no appointment and yet were still greeted warmly by the general manager, who had received notice from Mr. Bell that we might be stopping by.

He was a very tall, thin man, wearing a cream-colored cowboy hat, a chambray shirt tucked into blue jeans, a belt with a large silver buckle, and brown cowboy boots, all very Western looking. I thought to myself that this was just what Dennis would love to wear. He was a big fan of Westerns and absolutely loved belts and belt buckles. While that look would be out of place in England, it wasn't at all here in California.

The general manager led us to a golf cart – I did say Mondavi was large, didn't I? Away we went. It was a fascinating excursion, listening to all the details of the vineyard. Robert Mondavi was a much-loved pioneer in this region. He had used his technical abilities and marketing strategies to bring worldwide recognition to the wines of the Napa Valley. He single-handedly turned his passion for wine into a successful mainstream business and introduced a vast number of people across the world to wine. We ended our tour in the barrel room, an arched cave painted white, with a heavy planked wood table surrounded by Spanish-style wooden chairs. We sampled the wines and he indulged us with a tasting of a family reserve.

"This was truly a stupendous experience, and we could stay

forever. But we have another stop to make before it gets dark," I said to our host. We were just about to leave when another very tall man, also wearing a cowboy hat and a bolo tie, walked in. He was introduced as Robert Mondavi and I almost fell off my chair. Dennis and I looked at each other in disbelief. Could this day get any better?

"I hear you have come all the way from England," he said as he shook both our hands. He indulged us in a glass of the winery's Fumé Blanc and a story about its origins. "This was not always a popular variety," he said. "But in 1968, I made a dry oak–aged Sauvignon Blanc, and labeled it Fumé Blanc. The wine was a success. In time, Fumé Blanc became accepted as a synonym for Sauvignon Blanc." He then presented us with a couple of bottles of his most recent Fumé Blanc wine and excused himself. Once again, we experienced wonderful hospitality thanks to Mr. Bell.

A week later, as we traveled south toward Los Angeles, we stopped in Los Olivos and experienced the same hospitality at Firestone Vineyard. The general manager was dressed like the men at the Mondavi winery. He was heavier set but wore it well. *I must get Dennis a hat and belt*, I thought as we set out on an exclusive tour. It finished in a private tasting room where he had laid out some cheese and crackers and a whole line of wines ready for us to taste. The tasting room was newer, constructed all of wood. It reminded me of a barn, with really high ceilings and all the details that go into building a barn.

"Brooks Firestone is going to join us," he announced. And just then, as if on cue, Brooks entered the room. We made our pleas-antries, then we all sat down for an afternoon of drinking, tasting, eating, talking, and laughter. It was quite unreal, and it stunned me that they would take the time to entertain us as we were really strangers to them. But here we were, enjoying an intimate after-noon because of our association with Thornbury Castle, and they too were intrigued to know more about us, the castle, and Kenneth Bell. It was a fabulous experience.

Three hours later, we were back at our hotel in Santa Barbara. Much to our surprise, someone was in our room. What was happening, we wondered, as we rushed down to the receptionist. They were full of apologies. "We are not in the habit of going into someone's room," the manager said, very apologetic. "But we have an emergency and need to pack your belongings and change your room."

We soon learned what the emergency was. President Ronald Reagan, who had just been inaugurated earlier that year, was in town and security was tight. Secret Service agents were staying at our hotel and needed our room. To make amends, they upgraded us to one of their most luxurious and spacious suites.

"Let's stay in tonight, what do you say?" Dennis asked me.

"You don't need to twist my arm," I said, taking in the large bathtub, lush amenities, chandeliers, and amazing view. "We've got the Mondavi wine. Let's order room service."

Room service, like my first American breakfast, was indeed a revelation. So many firsts, and all of them with Dennis. That night we slept well before rolling into our next destination. Malibu, here we come.

Deviled Eggs with Caviar

Eggs on eggs ... two delicious tastes together! The eggs, blended with crème fraîche, Dijon mustard, white wine vinegar, and white pepper, get the final touch of decadence with caviar. Best served on toast points.

Serves 8

8 seven-minute boiled eggs, peeled
¼ cup crème fraîche
½ teaspoon white wine vinegar

1 teaspoon Dijon mustard
white pepper
1 ounce caviar

Cut the eggs in half lengthwise, removing the yolks to a medium bowl and placing the whites on a serving platter. Mash the yolks into a fine crumble using a fork. Add the crème fraiche, vinegar, mustard, and white pepper to taste, and mix well. In a piping bag with a medium nozzle, pipe the yolk mixture into the egg whites. Top with a ¼ teaspoon of caviar.

Cheesecake with Strawberry Sauce

This cheesecake is worth every calorie! It's a creamy New York style cheesecake served on a Graham Cracker crust and topped with a fresh strawberry sauce.

Serves 6

1 cup Graham Cracker crumbs

1½ tablespoons unsalted butter at
  room temperature

1½ tablespoons sugar, plus 1½ cups

2½ pounds cream cheese, softened

grated zest of 1 lemon

½ teaspoon vanilla extract

5 eggs

2 egg yolks

½ cup sour cream

1 teaspoon brandy

Preheat the oven to 375°F.

Butter the bottom of a 9-inch springform pan. In a mixing bowl, combine the Graham Cracker crumbs, butter, and 1½ tablespoons sugar and mix well. Press evenly onto the bottom of the springform pan and bake for about 8 minutes, until golden. Set aside and let cool. Lower the oven temperature to 350°F.

In a large mixing bowl with an electric mixer, combine the cream cheese, 1½ cups of sugar, lemon zest, and vanilla extract and beat until light and creamy. Add the eggs and yolks one at a time, mixing well after each addition. Add the sour cream and brandy and mix until smooth. Pour the mixture into the prepared pan. Wrap the pan in foil and place in a roasting pan. Fill the roasting pan with enough hot water to come halfway up the sides of the pan. Bake for about 1½ hours, until firm on the outside and not wobbly in the center.

Transfer the cheesecake to a cooling rack and let cool completely. Refrigerate overnight before serving.

Strawberry Sauce

2 pints fresh strawberries, sliced
½ cup sugar
1 cup water

1 teaspoon finely grated lemon zest
2 tablespoons of brandy

Combine the strawberries, sugar, water, and zest. Cook until the berries are soft and the liquid is thick, about 10 minutes. Stir in the brandy and cook for 1 minute. Remove from the heat and let cool. Spoon on top of the cheesecake and serve.

Ricotta Ravioli with Tomato Beurre Blanc Sauce

Just one of the many incredible dishes Dennis and I enjoyed in San Franciso, this ravioli can be a starter or a main course. The large ravioli is filled with a creamy ricotta mixture laced with a tomato beurre blanc and finished with a crispy basil leaf.

Serves 6

Tomato Beurre Blanc Sauce

¼ cup packed soft dried tomatoes
  (not packed in olive oil)
1½ sticks unsalted butter, softened
⅛ teaspoon kosher salt
⅓ cup minced shallots
⅔ cup dry white wine

3 tablespoons water
1 teaspoon fresh lemon juice
salt and freshly ground black pepper

You will also need:
plastic wrap

Soak the tomatoes in warm water for about 20 minutes, until softened. Drain and pat them dry, then mince. Combine the tomatoes, butter, and salt, form into a log shape, and cover with plastic wrap. Refrigerate until firm, then divide into 12 pieces.

Cook the shallots in one piece of tomato butter in a small heavy saucepan over moderate-low heat, stirring, for about 3 minutes, until softened. Add the wine and boil for about 10 minutes, until the liquid is reduced by half. Reduce the heat to low and whisk in the remaining cold tomato butter, one piece at a time, adding each piece before the previous one has completely melted and lifting the pan from the heat occasionally to cool the mixture (the sauce should not get hot enough to separate). Whisk in the water and lemon juice, then season to taste with salt and pepper.

Ravioli Dough

3¾ cups all-purpose flour
2 large eggs
2 egg yolks
1 tablespoon olive oil

You will also need:
plastic wrap

Mound the flour on a work surface and create a well in the center. Place the eggs, egg yolks, and olive oil in the well. Using a fork, whisk the eggs and oil together and slowly start dragging the flour into the egg mixture. Knead by hand until all the ingredients are well combined and the dough is smooth and elastic, about 10 minutes. Cover the dough with plastic wrap and let it rest at room temperature for at least 30 minutes.

Ravioli Filling

1 pound fresh ricotta, drain if wet
pinch of freshly grated nutmeg
1 teaspoon freshly grated lemon zest
(from about ½ a lemon)
1 cup freshly grated Parmigiano
Reggiano

1 large egg, plus one large egg lightly
beaten with two tablespoons water
kosher salt and freshly ground pepper

In a large bowl, combine the ricotta, nutmeg, lemon zest, Parmigiano Reggiano, and one egg. Season to taste with salt and pepper, stir well, and set aside.

Set up a pasta machine and turn it to the largest opening. Cut off pieces of dough about the size of an egg. Working with one piece at a time, roll the dough into sheets about ⅛ inch thick. Lay one pasta sheet on a lightly floured surface and cut two circles of the desired size of ravioli. Brush one circle with the lightly beaten egg mixture. Place a tablespoon of ricotta filling on the circle, top with the other circle, and seal the edges with your thumb or a fork. Repeat with the remaining pasta and filling.

When the beurre blanc sauce is nearly ready, bring a large pot of salted water to a boil. Add the ravioli and stir a few times to submerge and separate them. Cook uncovered at a gentle boil for 2–3 minutes, until the pasta is just tender to the bite. Drain the ravioli thoroughly.

To serve, place the ravioli in a bowl, pour the tomato beurre blanc sauce over the ravioli, and garnish with a crispy basil leaf.

John Dory Fillet with Lemon Beurre Blanc Sauce

Cooking at the time of our first trip to California was all about the sauces and fresh fish. The pan-fried fillets of John Dory are served with a lemony butter sauce with wilted garlic baby spinach.

Serves 6

John Dory Fillets

*12 skinless 4-ounce John Dory fillets
 (two per person)*
½ cup all-purpose flour
¼ cup of extra virgin olive oil

kosher salt and pepper
*6 thick slices of lemon dipped
 in chopped parsley on one side,
 for garnish*

Sift the all-purpose flour, seasoned to taste with salt and pepper, onto a plate. Heat the oil in a large heavy skillet over medium-high heat. Dredge the fish in the flour, shaking off the excess. Cooking in batches of four, add the fillets to the skillet and cook for about 3 minutes on each side, until golden on the outside and opaque in the center. Place in the oven on a low temperature to keep warm.

Lemon Beurre Blanc Sauce

1½ sticks unsalted butter, cut into 12 tablespoon sizes
⅓ cup minced shallots
⅔ cup dry white wine
⅛ teaspoon kosher salt
3 tablespoons water
1 teaspoon fresh lemon juice
salt and freshly ground black pepper

Melt one tablespoon of butter in a small heavy saucepan, add the shallots, and cook over moderate-low heat, stirring, for about 3 minutes, until softened. Add the wine and boil for about 10 minutes, until the liquid is reduced by half. Reduce the heat to low and whisk in the remaining cold butter, one piece at a time, adding each piece before the previous one has completely melted and lifting the pan from the heat occasionally to cool the mixture (the sauce should not get hot enough to separate). Whisk in the water and lemon juice, then season to taste with salt and pepper.

Wilted Baby Spinach

1 pound baby spinach, stems removed
1 stick unsalted butter
6 garlic cloves, finely chopped

kosher salt and freshly ground
black pepper

Melt the butter in a large skillet over medium-low heat, add the garlic, and cook for 1 minute to soften. Add the spinach and toss in the butter and garlic mixture until completely wilted. Season to taste with salt and pepper.

To serve, divide the wilted spinach between warm dinner plates, place two John Dory fillets on top, pour some lemon butter sauce over the fish, and garnish with a parsley-dipped lemon slice.

Venison in Red Wine Sauce
with Sweet Potato Herb Mash

One of the recipes in our marathon San Francisco experience, I'll never forget this roasted loin of venison served with a robust red wine sauce and a sweet potato herb mash.

Serves 4

Venison in Red Wine Sauce

2½ pounds venison loin

2 tablespoons malted milk powder

2 tablespoons poppy seeds

2 teaspoons finely chopped thyme

1½ teaspoons freshly ground black pepper

2 teaspoons kosher salt, plus more to taste

6 tablespoons unsalted butter

4 small shallots, peeled and cut into thin wedges

3 sprigs fresh thyme, plus extra to garnish

½ cup robust dry red wine

⅔ cup chicken stock

sprigs of fresh thyme, for garnish

Preheat the oven to 400°F.

In a small bowl, combine the malted milk powder, poppy seeds, thyme, and black pepper. Transfer the seasoning mixture to a large platter and roll the venison in the spices, patting the meat with your hands to help the seasonings to adhere. Let it rest for 10 minutes.

In a large ovenproof skillet, over medium heat, melt 4 tablespoons of the butter. Once hot and bubbling, add the venison loin and lower the heat slightly. Cook, rotating the meat one-quarter of the way every 3 minutes. Add the shallots and thyme to the pan, stirring briefly. Transfer the skillet to the oven and roast for about 10 minutes, or until a thermometer inserted into the thickest part of the meat reads 125°F. Transfer the venison to a platter and let it rest.

Meanwhile, place the skillet back over medium-high heat and add the red wine. Bring to a boil, then let cook for about 3 minutes, or until reduced by half. Add the chicken stock and bring the mixture back to a boil for about 1 minute. Add the remaining butter and cook, stirring, for about 2 minutes, until the butter is melted and the sauce thickens to the consistency of heavy cream. Stir in any juices that have accumulated on the venison platter.

Transfer the venison to a clean platter. Pour the sauce through a fine sieve and save it in a small bowl. Slice the venison in 1-inch medallions.

Sweet Potato Herb Mash

2 pounds sweet potatoes, peeled and
  diced
1 tablespoon finely chopped fresh
  thyme
1 tablespoon finely chopped rosemary

½ teaspoon kosher salt
¼ teaspoon cracked black pepper
1 stick unsalted butter, melted
4 tablespoons heavy cream

Fill a large saucepan with water and bring to a boil. Add the sweet potatoes, reduce to a simmer, and cook for about 30 minutes, or until they can be easily pierced with a knife. Drain the sweet potatoes and mash until they are lump free. Add the herbs, salt, pepper, melted butter, and cream. Mix until the potatoes have absorbed all the liquids.

Place a spoonful of sweet potato on each plate. Place the sliced venison medallions on top of the mash and ladle the sauce over the meat. Garnish with a fresh thyme sprig.

CHAPTER THIRTEEN

Burgers and Beaches

After saying a fond goodbye to the quaint beauty of Santa Barbara with a coffee and pastry on the pier, we were back on the road heading to Malibu. On the way, we took the two-lane highway that ran parallel to the coast. Driving through myriad strawberry fields, we found ourselves recapping our trip and all that we had experienced.

I couldn't get over the weather and the scenery and the fact that we could find such fabulous food any time of the day or night. "And the people!" I exclaimed. "Remember the night we got lost in Half Moon Bay and stumbled into that bar that also had rooms for let? Then there was that man willing to give you his cowboy boots simply because you said you liked them and then wanted to drive us to the finest restaurant in town?"

We both laughed, thinking back to these recent fond moments. As we turned onto Pacific Coast Highway from the farm road we were on, I stopped cold. The view of the Pacific Ocean appearing out of nowhere took my breath away. "Wow," I sighed. "And let's not forget the incredible weather, the blue skies, and that sparkling ocean!"

"Yep," Dennis agreed. "It gets me every time. What's not to like about California?" he said, taking my hand across the seats and giving me an irresistible smile.

"We have a lot to think about, Dennis. But honestly, I could live anywhere in the world with you by my side. You give me strength, love, and the feeling we can conquer anything together." And yet, in the back of my mind, I knew things would not be easy to arrange, should we go forward. There were still the children to think about before we could decide anything.

I let that thought go for the moment as we were entering Malibu. "So, this is the famous Malibu," I said as we passed a sign telling us how many people lived there and that it was twenty-seven miles long. "Gosh, it's that big? I had no idea." Dennis was playing tour guide, giving me the commentary of what we were driving by. We were heading toward the heart of Malibu and along the way there was a lot to see... or rather, not see. Celebrities might live here, but they have done a great job of hiding their homes from the highway with dense foliage, long driveways, and formidable stone and iron gates.

"Over there is Broad Beach, where the rich and famous live." Dennis pointed to a strip of homes along the water. "And see that restaurant over there? That's where I sometimes meet Craig and the boys for breakfast. We see Dustin Hoffman having breakfast there a lot."

I nodded, thinking of how fun it was to be talking about celebrities. How far removed this was from our world in England! I also discovered the reason Dennis didn't pick up my call from the airport. He and John were with Stevie Nicks and Mick Fleetwood in Beverly Hills the night before. I was impressed, and soon to be even more so. The house next door to John and Hannah was owned by Don Henley of the Eagles and that was where he wrote "Hotel California." And Barbra Streisand was building five homes on one property down the road with Jon Peters. One day she had given Dennis a ride in her convertible Rolls-Royce to show him around two of the houses. "What?" I couldn't believe it. "Surely you are joking?" Dennis just shook his head and laughed.

As we passed a large stretch of beach, the narration continued. "This is Zuma Beach, where the surfing world championships take place." As we drove up the hill, he pointed to a little shop. "That's where I go on Tuesday mornings to get freshly baked donuts and coffee for everyone." At this, he paused and after some thought he said, smiling, "You know, if we end up not staying in America, I think I would miss the coffee and donuts ritual." I had to laugh and now I wanted to try those donuts more than anything.

Just then, we turned right off the highway. He pulled the car over and stopped. "This is the tunnel I walk through every time I go to the Paradise Cove Inn," he said, pointing toward the ocean. "That's where they film *The Rockford Files*. I'll take you down there tomorrow." We continued through the tunnel onto a private road. There were no sidewalks. The road simply butted right up to gardens. Some had fences, but many didn't. The area looked very rustic and raw, but it had an untouched natural charm about it.

Dennis stopped the car in the middle of the road and pointed up the hill. "That's where I live, up there." We continued up the road, which was now dirt. He had told me about this in letters. There were two trailers – a larger one for John and Hannah and their family and the small one-room trailer Dennis lived in. We would have called it a "caravan" in England. It certainly wasn't as fancy as he thought it would be. It was a disappointment for him, but life sometimes throws a curve ball, and you have to get on with your lot, as my dad would say. Pick your battles. Dennis had picked his battles and for now, the accommodation was something that he just got on with.

I had been feeling nervous about meeting Hannah and John

but there really was no need. They were lovely and immediately made me feel comfortable. John's parents were also there and both extremely down to earth. It felt as if we all knew each other already. I am sure Dennis chewed their ears off about me along the way. It was like we were one big happy family and had just come home after a long trip.

We hung around and chatted, had a cup of tea, and Dennis and John went off talking "shop," walking around the property while Hannah and the parents got to know me better. It was painless and conversation flowed as we talked about this and that, my family, the project, Joanne and Ross. They had nothing but praise for Dennis, saying how much they liked working with him. When Dennis and John returned, John suggested champagne. "To properly welcome you to California, Pauline." And so that was how it all started, with one big celebration. I had to LOVE that!

We stayed in Malibu for three days. We were staying at the Tonga Lei, a Polynesian-style hotel with a bamboo fence and tiki torches lining the entrance. Inside, the restaurant was divided by woven-style curtains to create private seating areas, with a table and two bench seats in each area. The Tonga Lei was one of two motels in Malibu, the other being the Surfrider, across from the pier. It was certainly unlike anything I had ever seen.

My first impression of Malibu was that it wasn't pretty. We had just driven Highway 1, where everything was beautiful and untouched. I felt a little disappointed when I got there and PCH was lined with what I'd call shanty homes. They were so close together you couldn't see the ocean. Overhead billboards and broken-down signs cut into the blue sky. *There must be something to the place*, I thought. *How could it have become so well known?* I decided to reserve judgment for the moment.

As promised, Dennis took me to Paradise Cove, where I ate my first American burger. I know it seems unreal, but I had never had a hamburger before, ever! It was so big I could hardly get it in my mouth! "Everything in America is so big," I murmured. Apart from the pickles, which I didn't like and removed, it was delicious.

As always in America, there were options when ordering the burger. I could choose fruit, French fries, or crunchy onion rings. I decided on onion rings. They were coated in a seasoned crunchy batter and came with ketchup and a ranch dressing, which I'd never had before. I fell in love with ranch dip and completely indulged with the irresistible onion rings.

Another new food I experienced in Malibu was sushi. John and Hannah were big fans of it, so they ordered for us when we went out to a place in Zuma that was supposed to be the best. Dennis loved it but I was dubious. After much trial and error, I realized it was the nori flavor I didn't like because I loved sashimi, which is served very pure with a light ponzu sauce and crispy wontons.

We ventured over to Pacific Palisades, which we loved for its cute village. From there we continued driving on Sunset Boulevard through Beverly Hills and into Hollywood. What a contrast in environment from the pristine manicured roads lined with palm trees of Beverly Hills. We could immediately feel the change as we drove into Hollywood. There was no greenery and the streets were crowded, with billboards, souvenir shops and people selling road maps to the stars, nightclubs, theaters, tall buildings, restaurants. "What a contrast from Beverly Hills to Hollywood, uh?" I said as I stared at a scantily clad street performer and the crowd who was taking pictures of her.

Back in Malibu, we breathed a sigh of relief from the craziness of Hollywood. We dined at Alice's at the entrance to the pier, which, luckily for us, was right next to Tonga Lei. We had learned that you need a car in Malibu. Everything is so spread out. But tonight, fortunately, we were within walking distance. Alice's was a small restaurant that had quite a following. It was hard to get a reservation so people would come and wait up to two hours or more for a table. Fortunately, our hotel made a reservation for us. We had a table for two outside on the pier deck overlooking the ocean waves and were able to watch the surfers. All quite perfect, especially as the sun was about to set.

We had another first experience when we ordered margaritas. It sounded great but I wasn't sure if I was a citrus-in-my-drink kind of girl. Dennis had his shaken and served on the rocks. I ordered mine straight up in a margarita glass. "These glasses are fun," I said, still absolutely delighted by everything I found in California by way of hospitality and service. I took a sip and instantly loved it. I was a citrus girl! More than that, I loved the tequila. I had never had it until now. Learning that, the waiter proceeded to give me a brief education and brought me a shot of silver tequila. I was smitten.

Looking over the sparkling ocean, feeling the California sunshine and enjoying these new flavors, was just what we needed. "Well, this is all quite magical," I sighed. "Do you think I love everything so much because we are on vacation and we're on this romantic journey together? Would we feel the same if we were living here or would all the magic go away?" I mused.

"Well, how many vacations have you had that you've loved but also thought, I could really live here?" Dennis pondered.

"Hmm. A few, I think," I said, laughing. "But there is something in the air here, isn't there? There's such good energy. Or is that my imagination?"

"I know what you mean, Peeps, I feel the same. Maybe it's the weather? It makes people warm, friendly, upbeat, and positive," he said. I had to agree.

But the larger question was not about margaritas, friendly people, or weather. It was about our work. I had to be sure to ask the right questions, so I asked Dennis what he thought of his opportunities here. Did he see them for himself, and for me? "I do," he said without hesitation. "The job is right up my street and I'm certain I can find more work when it's done."

"So, we'd be emigrating then, not just staying for the duration of the job?"

He nodded his head, wondering what I really thought. I put his worries at bay, saying happily, "Well, you know me, always up for an adventure!" And yes, I was on my second margarita!

"But seriously," I said as I reached out to hold his hand, "if we make this move, I think we should think long term. It's too big of an upheaval to go back to England after three years. We'd have to start all over again. It's not like we're working for a large corporation, and we aren't getting any younger." I paused to think about what I would say next. "If we can get the legal papers to come here, get sole custody of Joanne and Ross, then let's do it."

He looked at me with a sort of surprised shock, as much as to say, *We are doing this?* But I had one more important question. "If we can't get sole custody but we can get the legal papers, would you want to stay to complete the project or come back to England after six months?" I breathed a sigh of relief when he answered, "No, I couldn't stay here by myself. My life would be nothing without you, Joanne and Ross. I'd come back to England and start our life together."

I smiled. "Then, let's toast." I raised my glass. "California, here we come!" And just like that, it was done. We'd made the decision. We both sat back in our chairs in disbelief, looking at each other, our minds quietly working overtime, reflecting on what we needed to do to really make all this happen. I broke the silence and asked the last, truly most important question. "What shall we eat?"

We smiled at each other, opening the menu to indulge once again in our favorite pastime of eating. Dennis took a quick look at the menu and said, "Let's have the tacos, I think you'll like them.

I had them once with John on an outing in Santa Monica." Decision made, another new experience, eating a taco. I loved it!

We were on the last leg of our trip to San Diego the next morning. Dennis was driving and I was the navigator. I was concentrating on making sure we got onto the right freeways. Once we got on the 405, I could relax a bit as it was a straight shot. These long car rides had been perfect for all the planning we had to do.

Dennis opened this one with a biggie. "When do you think we should get married?"

"How about when you come home at Christmas?"

Dennis nodded and said, "That means you'll be planning by yourself."

"Darling, I'm a professional, remember?" I said, laughing. "Besides, it'll be a small wedding, right?"

"Yes, I think so, just family and a few friends."

"We're on the same page then. Love that!"

We decided Dennis would come home on December 18 and we would plan to have the wedding in the late morning of December 22, followed by a lunch reception. Those few days would give him enough time to get over jet lag and pick up anything extra he would need. Dennis would oversee the honeymoon, which we'd take in Bath, England's most charming Georgian city, named after the Roman-built baths.

We had been deep in wedding reverie when I looked up from my map. "Oh dear, I think we're lost," I said, looking around. We'd somehow left the main road and it looked like we were going through an orange grove. There was no real road, nor roads on the map to guide us out. For a moment, I was a little scared. We'd been traveling on this road for an hour and hadn't seen a soul and we were getting low on gas. Just then we saw a break in the trees, and it took us out to what looked like a new housing estate being built.

"Wow, I thought for a moment we'd be lost in the orange

groves forever and have to cancel the wedding," I said, smiling as I looked over at Dennis. I had expected perhaps a bit of irritation from him. But there was nothing. He stayed totally calm. We saw a shop ahead of us to get water and to find out exactly where we were. As we got out of the car, the heat hit us like a thunderbolt. "Argh, how hot is it?" The gauge on the shop said 109 degrees. "Gosh, does Malibu get hot like this? Maybe we need to reconsider living here!" I said jokingly. "Come on, let's find the hotel. I've seen enough orange groves."

We spent a couple of fun days in San Diego experiencing the beaches, Gaslamp Quarter, and Channel Harbor, with many dining interludes. But sadly it was time to leave and for me to get back to England. On the morning we had to get to the airport, I woke to find Dennis gone. I hadn't heard him leave. I got a little bit of a chill until I saw him at the door, holding a tray with coffee, orange juice, a champagne split, croissants, and a bud vase with a carnation. "How did you get this? I didn't see room service or a café in this hotel."

"I asked the cleaning lady to put it together for me," he smiled, and gave me a kiss. "I wanted to do something special before we left. I know I don't have a ring, but I want you to know I love you with all my heart. You make me so happy, and the thought of spending the rest of my life with you overwhelms me," he said. "Truly, I love you, Peeps, and I can't imagine life without you, Joanne and Ross. For the third time, will you marry me?"

No answer was needed, the kiss said it all. Starting the day with a marriage proposal is quite special, ring or no ring, and I thought sealing the deal with another lovely meal was quite appropriate for the two of us. We were both on cloud nine. Making all those big decisions was scary, but we both knew we were doing the right thing. Getting married and starting a life in California was the plan. Now we just had to tell the world about our love.

We decided to tell our parents first and they could spread the news to the family. My mum answered the phone.

"Mum, it's Pauline. Do you want some exciting news?"

"Always," she said.

"Dennis asked me to marry him, and I said yes."

"Oh Pauline, that is wonderful news! Wait until I tell your father. He'll be thrilled. When will it be?" she asked.

"Dennis will come home at Christmas, so we thought that timing would be perfect. Anyway, Mum, we're calling from California, which is costing us a fortune. I'll catch up with all the details when I get home tomorrow. There's so much to talk about."

"Have a safe trip. Oh, I'm so excited for you, can't wait to see you," she said as we hung up.

It was now Dennis's turn to tell his parents, but unfortunately the reaction was not the same. They were very disappointed that he was choosing to marry a divorcee, and one with children at that. I believe the word "gold digger" had come up, which if it wasn't so hurtful would have been something to laugh about. The most hurtful thing, though, was that they refused to attend the wedding. Dennis was heartbroken and hung up the phone very slowly.

I thought he was going to cry, but he just put his arms around me until I finally had to move away and look at him seriously. "They don't approve of me?"

"It seems that way," he said. "But we're getting married regardless."

I flew out of Los Angeles with mixed emotions of fear, happiness, loneliness, optimism, sadness, and excitement. Once again, I found myself with tears streaming down my cheeks as I boarded the plane. I took one more look back at Dennis before he went out of sight. "I hope you'll be alright. I love you," I said to myself.

Margarita

Is there any better way to have a margarita than in Malibu, looking out over the ocean with the man you love? That was my first experience with this drink and it (and tequila) quickly became my favorite! This margarita is made with Reposado tequila shaken with orange liqueur, agave nectar, and freshly squeezed lime juice, served in a glass with a salt rim and a fresh lime wheel. It's best enjoyed with friends, which is why I'm giving you my recipe for a pitcher as well as a single drink!

For a Single Margarita

lime wedge, for glass rim
coarse salt, for glass rim
1½ ounces silver tequila
1 ounce orange liqueur (Cointreau,
  Grand Marnier or triple sec)

¾ ounce freshly squeezed lime juice
agave syrup, to taste
lime wheel, for garnish

Run a lime wedge around the rim of your serving glass. Place coarse salt on a plate and dip your glass into the salt to coat the rim. Add the tequila, orange liqueur, lime juice, and a few ice cubes to a cocktail shaker. Shake until well combined. Give it a taste and add agave nectar if you would like it to be sweeter.

Fill a glass with ice cubes and pour in the margarita mix. Garnish with a lime wheel.

A Pitcher of Margaritas
(16 Servings)

lime wedges, for glass rim
coarse salt, for glass rim
2 cups of Reposado tequila
2 cups orange liqueur

1½ cups freshly squeezed lime juice
agave syrup, to taste
limes wheels, for garnish

Classic Beef Steak Hamburger

Truth be told, I LOVE a simple no-fuss thick juicy fatty hamburger. Why fatty? For one, the taste and texture are fabulous with champagne and two, the fat gives the burger a beautiful char on the outside.

Serves 4

2 pounds 80 percent lean and
  20 percent fat ground chuck
cheddar cheese slices
kosher salt and freshly ground
  black pepper

To serve:
4 sesame seed hamburger buns
Dijon mustard
ketchup
romaine lettuce leaves
beefsteak tomato slices
red onion, thinly sliced
avocado slices

Preheat the grill to 400°F.

Place the beef in a large bowl and sprinkle with salt and pepper to taste. Use your hands to mix the seasoning until well combined. Divide the meat mixture into fourths. Using your hands, press each fourth into the shape of a hamburger patty, about 1 inch thick. Make an indentation in the center of the patty to prevent it bulging as it cooks.

Place the burgers on the grill – either charcoal or gas – and cook for 3–4 minutes on one side. Flip the burgers over and cook for a further 3–4 minutes, until the burgers have reached the desired doneness. I usually cook for 4 minutes on each side for medium well done burgers, which is 160°F if using a meat thermometer.

If adding cheese, lay a slice on each burger for about a half minute to let it slightly melt. Serve the burgers on hamburger buns with Dijon mustard, ketchup, lettuce, tomato, onion, and avocado.

Onion Rings with Ranch Dip

Burgers were a revelation to me when I had my first one at Paradise Cove in Malibu. But the true star of the day was the onion ring. The Ranch Dip was quite a surprise addition and so very American. I can't eat onion rings any other way now.

2 large white onions, peeled
6 cups ice water
2 cups all-purpose flour
1 teaspoon coarse salt, plus extra for
  sprinkling

¼ teaspoon white pepper
½ teaspoon baking powder
1 cup beer, lager or pilsner
2 tablespoons ice water
canola oil, for frying

Peel and cut the onions crosswise into ½-inch slices. Separate into rings and place in a large bowl with the 6 cups of ice water while you prepare the batter.

In a medium mixing bowl, whisk together half the flour with the salt, white pepper, and baking powder. Whisk in the beer and the 2 tablespoons of ice water until just combined

In a large pot over medium-high heat, heat 3 inches of oil to 375°F.

Place the remaining flour in a separate bowl. Remove the rings from the ice water bath and pat dry. Coat the rings first in the flour then in the batter, allowing any excess to drip off.

Working in batches, transfer the battered rings to the hot oil and cook for 2–3 minutes, or until golden brown. Transfer to a rack lined with paper towels to drain. Sprinkle with salt.

Homemade Ranch Dip

½ cup good-quality mayonnaise

½ cup sour cream

½ cup buttermilk

3 tablespoons minced fresh parsley

1½ teaspoons minced fresh dill

½ teaspoon apple cider vinegar

½ teaspoon Worcestershire sauce

½ teaspoon garlic powder

¼ teaspoon onion powder

¼ teaspoon salt

freshly cracked black pepper

In a medium bowl, whisk together the mayonnaise, sour cream, and buttermilk until smooth. Stir in the parsley, dill, vinegar, Worcestershire sauce, garlic powder, onion powder, salt, and pepper to taste. Blend well and adjust the seasonings to taste.

Cover and refrigerate for at least 4 hours or overnight. If the consistency is too thick, thin with an additional splash of buttermilk.

Seafood Tacos

Fish tacos put California beach food on the map. They are delicious with a marinated grilled flaky cod served in a corn tortilla with avocado. I add purple corn slaw with sour cream and a squeeze of fresh lime juice, in true San Diego style!

Serves 8

Tacos

1½ *pounds cod or other flaky*
   white fish
3 *tablespoons extra virgin olive oil*
juice of 1 lime
2 *teaspoons chili powder*
1 *teaspoon paprika*
½ *teaspoon cayenne pepper*
½ *teaspoon ground cumin*

½ *tablespoon vegetable oil*
kosher salt and freshly ground pepper

To serve:
8 *corn tortillas*
1 *avocado, diced*
8 *lime wedges*
sour cream

In a medium shallow bowl, whisk together the olive oil, lime juice, chili powder, paprika, cayenne, and cumin. Add the cod, tossing until evenly coated. Let marinate for 15 minutes.

Heat the vegetable oil in a large nonstick skillet over medium heat. Remove the cod from the marinade and season both sides of each fillet with salt and pepper. Add the fish to the skillet, flesh side down. Cook until opaque and cooked through, 3–4 minutes per side. Let it rest for 5 minutes and lightly flake with a fork.

Corn Slaw

¼ cup mayonnaise
juice of 1 lime
2 tablespoons fresh chopped cilantro
1 teaspoon honey

2 cups shredded purple cabbage
1 cup corn kernels
1 jalapeño, finely minced
salt and freshly ground black pepper

Make the slaw while the fish is marinating. In a large bowl, whisk together the mayonnaise, lime juice, cilantro, and honey. Stir in the cabbage, corn, and jalapeño. Season to taste with salt and pepper.

Serve the fish over grilled corn tortillas with the corn slaw and diced avocado. Squeeze lime juice over everything and finish with a dollop of sour cream.

CHAPTER FOURTEEN
Back to Reality

Settling into my plane seat for the long trip back to England, I took out the notepad and pen I had bought in the gift shop. There were a lot of arrangements to make, and my mind was swirling. I got as far as writing "Wedding List" at the top of the page before leaning my head back with my thoughts. I realized I hadn't fully taken in what had just happened. The trip had been wildly romantic, life-changing to say the least, with not only a wedding to plan but the details of moving to another country to sort out. It doesn't get more exciting – or frightening – than that. However, it was all so bittersweet. Dennis and I would be torn apart again for a little while, and he and his family might be torn apart forever.

I closed my eyes for a moment. A "moment" turned into a few hours and when I woke, I was well rested. We were about to land at Heathrow. I had decided that the first thing I wanted to do was to tell my parents about our plans to move to America, and would drive straight to their home to tell them firsthand. I'd hate it if they heard through the grapevine.

As I pulled up, Dad was puttering in the garden. He was surprised to see me but welcomed me with open arms. "I just couldn't wait to tell you about my trip," I said, while admiring his dahlias.

"Let's go find your mum and put the kettle on."

Mum was listening to the BBC News on the radio at the kitchen table. She looked up as I came through the back door and immediately turned off the radio. Dad came in and we settled around the kitchen table with a cup of tea. "I'm going to get right to the point," I said.

They looked at me expectantly, wondering what on earth I could say that would top the wedding news. I took a deep breath and began. "Not only have Dennis and I decided to get married…" I took a pause, staring at the ground for what seemed like forever. I was having trouble getting the words out. I looked up and said, "We have decided to take the steps to emigrate to America." The silence that followed also seemed to last forever. My mum spoke first.

"Oh my," was all she said.

My dad sat forward in his chair. Cigarette in hand, he took a puff, blew out the smoke, waited for a second, and said, "This is a bit of a shock. But I suppose by now I should know you aren't a girl who sits back and lets life take you. You've always had that sense of adventure for greater things." He smiled for a moment and chuckled, "Dennis has got his hands full." Then he added, "You are both hard workers and I know you'll have success in whatever you decide to tackle. We support anything that makes you happy in life, even though we'll be very sad and miss you." Then, looking at Mum, he said, "We are losing our big baby."

Later that night, my dad took me aside. I'd never had a heart-to-heart with him about my ambitions but I think he realized that I was starting to see a larger picture for myself.

"You know, Pauline, there are always times when opportunities will come up. Some are good, some aren't. You've always had keen instincts, from the move to Blostin's, then to the castle, and

I trust you know that this move will be a good one for you and the children too."

"Thanks, Dad." I was trying not to tear up. "You and Mum have always believed in me. From you I get the strength to work through the challenges that come with that to achieve what I want."

It was funny – the list he rattled off wasn't of "dreams" I'd had as a child or even as a young woman. They were, as he so rightly stated, opportunities. And once I start down the road of an opportunity, then I do my best to make it successful. In the back of my mind, I believe it's better to have tried and failed than not to have tried at all. What is life without risk? If I hadn't taken risks, I might have still been living with a man who didn't love me and with no future to mold and nurture.

After a few tears, the conversation quickly became one of excitement and happiness. Together, we raised question after question. Some we had answers for. Many we didn't. I certainly didn't know what would happen with the children. And although my parents were sad that we'd be so far away, they gave me their blessing. They were extremely happy for us at the thought of what lay ahead in this new adventure of ours.

I arrived home later that night after staying with Mum and Dad for dinner. Joanne and Ross had been with David and he would be dropping them off the next day.

As I was unpacking, I wondered if I should say anything just yet to Joanne and Ross. Or to David. I was not looking forward to that conversation. It would have to happen sooner rather than later since we still needed to get papers to be in America and I had to get sole custody of the children. Of course, none of this might happen, but I had to do my best to make it so.

I went right back to my letter-writing routine and got into bed with my red wine, pen and paper, and started to write my love letter to Dennis. There was so much to say already, and we had only been apart for twenty-four hours! But my big news tonight was to let him know Mum and Dad approved and were so happy for us. I fell asleep before I finished.

I had missed Joanne and Ross terribly and kept watch out the castle window for them. As David's car turned into the gravel drive, I went downstairs to greet them at the castle entrance. As soon as they saw me, Joanne and Ross burst into smiles and were anxious to get out of the car. They raced to give me a huge hug, wrapping their arms around my legs and pressing their heads into my thighs, one on either side. I bent down to hug them, saying through my tears how much I'd missed them. I really didn't realize how much I'd missed them. With all that had happened, it felt like we'd been apart a lifetime. Wiping the tears aside, I said, "Come on, let's get you inside. I might be able to find a present from America. Daddy, can you bring up the suitcases?" I took each of their hands and we walked up the stairs together.

This was not the time to talk to David about our trip to America and what our intentions were. I would do that another time. Joanne and Ross started to tell me what they had been doing and David interjected with details. They had gone with Sue, Vicki, and Matthew to Cornwall. It sounded like they had a fabulous time, even though the weather was not that great. After I got all the news of the vacation, David picked them up, giving them a kiss goodbye. "Be good for your mum, and I will see you again next week," he said as he left.

While I bathed them, I told them about America. "It's so big there. Dennis lives in a funny little house overlooking the ocean. I ate something called a hamburger." And on and on until their five- and six-year-old minds turned to other things.

It always surprised me how well they transitioned from me to David and vice versa. Maybe we were lucky. They had each other, which I think was part of the reason. Also, they had known Sue and her children, Vicki and Matthew, before the divorce, so it was perhaps a little more seamless than if they had to meet a completely new family.

Of course, they would tell me Daddy would let them do this and that if I wouldn't let them do something, but David and I worked really hard at communicating and supporting each other over such situations.

"Is Dennis coming back?" Joanne asked as I scrubbed behind her ears.

"Yes, he'll be back for Christmas. Would you like that?"

"Yes," she said. Neither of them seemed overly interested but they did listen to me.

"OK, the fun is over. Out you come," I said, wrapping Ross in a towel.

I had thought about setting them down that night to tell them how Dennis and I were in love and were going to get married. But during their bath, I realized they probably didn't need to know the full scope of the situation. After all, why get them all worked up when Dennis wasn't going to be back for another four months?

Back at work, we were now operating at full speed to transform the castle into a seven-room hotel. Mr. Bell and Molly were out and about buying furniture, paintings, and curtains. They were fully enjoying the experience of designing the rooms.

As they focused on that, my work duties increased. It was exciting and I loved every minute of it, although it was quite exhausting, working and being a mother, but it all came together. It was just a case of staying organized and being on top of things. Besides, I was feeling really happy about all the prospects going on in my life, which kept me in full spirits, and also it was not giving me much of a chance to think and miss Dennis too much.

When I told Mr. Bell that Dennis and I were getting married, he immediately offered the castle for the reception. I was speechless and grateful. "Good, good," he said, happy that he could do this for me. "Let me know what you'd like for the menu. I can choose some wines for you."

Never in my dreams could I have imagined a better place for our reception. We were going to have the actual ceremony at the registry office in Bristol. I had already decided I didn't want to wear a wedding dress, just a very smart dress and a hat. With those very large elements of the wedding sorted out, I turned my attention to the cake.

I would make and serve a traditional fruitcake covered with marzipan and royal icing. Fruitcakes were traditional not only for weddings but also for Christmas, and since our wedding would take place at Christmas, I thought it the perfect choice. My special recipe would take months to prepare between all the candied and dried fruit, as well as infusing the cake with brandy and letting the flavor mature, so I'd start on it soon. I'd make the marzipan and icing the week before.

I was still writing a letter a day to Dennis and getting one from him. This was truly precious. I even read parts of his letters to Joanne and Ross to keep him in their minds. On one of those occasions, I found myself telling them that I loved him, just like I loved them, and that I missed him just like I missed them when they left to go somewhere.

Before I knew it, I was slowly telling them about the wedding. "When he comes back from America at Christmas, we're getting married. Joanne, we'd like you to be our bridesmaid. And, Ross, you'll be our page boy. And when we're married, he will be living with us all the time, won't that be fun?" The reaction was "Yes, great." That was it. No therapist, no tears, and they looked at me as much as to say, *now can we play?* Job done!

A week or so after returning to England, I had to seek a solicitor so I could apply for sole custody. I had no idea how long the process would take or if we would have to go to court. After calling David to talk to him, it was clear it would be the latter. He was furious and his words rang in my ears: "I will do everything in my power to stop you from taking the children out of the country." Shortly after that, we were assigned to a social worker to investigate our case.

Of course, this caused a lot of tension between us. We had to hide this uncomfortable situation and emotion from the children. That took some acting, but I think we did an OK job. Drop-offs and pickups got a lot faster, that's for sure.

In all honesty, I truly felt sorry about the situation with David. He was a good father. Our divorce had been painless once I got over the hurt, and we had developed some harmony between us regarding the children. I wasn't doing this out of spite, I said again and again. It just happened. I never thought in a million years I would be thinking about living in America or that I'd be getting married before Sue and David.

It wasn't long before I was driving to the airport again to pick up Dennis. I thought of all the twists and turns from that moment when I learned about Sue and David. At that time, I thought I'd never get over the pain or humiliation and now, here I am, about to take off for a new chapter of my life. I had butterflies at the thought of seeing Dennis again.

I always love the arrivals gate at customs. There is a palpable sense of excitement in the air. I watched as, one by one, couples were reunited with long kisses, grandparents and grandchildren exchanged gifts and hugs, and husbands waited with airport-bought bouquets of flowers for their wives.

The crowd was beginning to thin out and I wondered if I'd missed him. I turned around to check the corridors and when I turned back, there he was. I realized there was no way I could have missed him. He was walking out alone, a big smile on his face. He was taller, leaner, and more tanned than I remembered. California was indeed a bit of magic. It was eighty-four degrees when Dennis left California and it was minus nine degrees that day in England.

I was bundled up from head to toe so I wouldn't be jumping over any ropes to greet him. Instead, I waited for what seemed an eternity for him to get to me, but soon enough we were in each other's arms again. The loving kiss was worth the wait.

The cold air hit us hard as we left the terminal. "Damn, I left your jacket in the car," I said. We ran to the car to get warm again. "Can't say I've missed this!" he said as he closed the car door.

I waited until we'd navigated the airport confusion and were on the M4 before bringing up the wedding. Looking over at him, it felt like no time had passed at all. "I hate to bombard you with all that we have to do for the wedding, but we only have three days to get everything done," I said.

"As long as I can go to the pub tonight and have a pint, I'll be good to go," he said. "Now THAT I have missed!"

"More than me?" I said, batting my eyelashes.

"Oh, my goodness, no!" he replied.

"Ah, good answer," I said, smiling.

I was taking the week before the wedding off from work and we were all staying at my parents'. Silly as it might sound, my mum asked if Dennis and I could sleep in separate rooms. She thought it was unlucky to sleep together in the same room before the wedding. I had to laugh, but I understood. Traditions are important when it comes to weddings. Besides, after months apart, another night or two would only make our wedding night so much sweeter.

The next three days were intense. I had my outfit and Joanne and Ross were all set too. But Dennis still had to get his suit, tie, shirt, and shoes, which we accomplished in one hit at Brooks

Brothers at the top of Park Street. My Aunty Audrey guided me to a jewelry wholesaler where we got our nine-carat gold bands with no adjustments needed. Check, check!

We visited the castle to confirm we had twenty-five guests and to go through the seating plan. Fernando had the cake. On the day, he'd place a simple bud vase with carnation flowers on the top. Mr. Bell had printed a menu card for each guest with a painting of the castle skyline on one side. We had arranged for Tony the pianist to play during lunch, so I let Fernando know those details. *We are on a roll*, I thought to myself.

However, amid our happiness there was one lingering point of sadness. Dennis was heartbroken that his parents continued to be adamant he was making the wrong choice. He'd written them several letters and even called a few times from the States to talk to them. I had also written to them, explaining that we loved each other very much and that I'd never hurt him. We later learned that letter only added fuel to the fire. "How dare she send me a letter like that?" his father had said. We also learned later that his older brother had called me "a gold-digging divorcee with loose morals and two children." That stung a bit, but I attributed it to the fact that one, they didn't know me at all, and two, they were old fashioned. A woman working in the hospitality industry, or perhaps a woman working at all, was suspect to them.

Even with all of this, Dennis and I took one more trip to Shepton Mallet to ask them in person to come to the wedding. I waited in the car to give Dennis and his parents as much family time as needed. When he came out after forty-five minutes, his face said it all. As he started the engine, his first words were simply, "Let's not talk about this anymore. I've done everything I can to get them to understand, but they've chosen not to. I love you. I want to marry you and spend the rest of my life with you, so we have to move on."

"I'm so sorry, Dennis," I said, kissing him on the cheek before we started to drive back to my parents' home, where the atmosphere could not have been more different.

As we arrived, we could hear laughter, conversations, and children playing before we even got to the door. How different from the silence at the Parrys' house. Lesley and Pascal had arrived from Paris. Lesley is my youngest sister. She left home at eighteen, bound for France and a job as an au pair. After meeting and marrying Pascal, she settled in Paris and never came back to England. They married in Bouges-le-Château, a village in the Berry region in central France, where Pascal lived growing up. Their wedding took place in an amazing château. The wedding meal was a marathon feast with course after course being served – our eyes grew bigger every time they placed a plate of food. Our glasses were kept filled with Chateaumeillant, a nice local red wine. True to French style, they had a traditional croquembouche for the wedding cake.

Lesley opened the door to us, and Joanne and Ross came running out. "What a wonderful welcome," I said as I gave Lesley a hug. I reached down to kiss Joanne and Ross.

We had so much to catch up on. We all gathered around the dining room table. Lesley and Pascal had brought the wine. I had given Joanne and Ross their bath early so they could join us for dinner. It wouldn't hurt for them to go to bed a little later than normal.

Mum had made us a lovely rosemary roast leg of lamb with roast potatoes, carrots, and mint sauce. There were also green beans from their summer crop, which had been frozen together with sweet peas. "This is wonderful, I've so missed roast dinners like this!" Dennis said, and we all laughed. It's true, there's not much better than a roast.

For dessert we had a rustic apple crumble with thick pouring cream. There was a lot of talk and excitement about the wedding and we found ourselves looking back at Lesley and Pascal's wedding, just over a year ago. "I can't believe after your wedding, Les, two o'clock in the morning, we went to that bar and you were still in your wedding dress drinking John Courage beer followed by multiple vodka shots!" Oh my, that was something. I'm not sure how we all got up the next day.

But we did, thanks to Dad coming around the hotel banging on everyone's door. "I remember that day around the lake. I couldn't get enough of the Galette aux Pommes de Terre," I said, always one to remember the menu more than anyone else did. "It was a perfect bite of comfort that helped soak up the night-before indulgences. I think I must have had a dozen or more," I said, laughing. That galette, I learned later, was a local specialty, precooked slices of potato and fresh cream served in a flaky pastry square.

Our dinner and the family laughter were just what Dennis needed to distract him from his own family's nonsense earlier that day. But we weren't done yet. After dinner, Dad got up from the table. "Who's coming to the pub?" My dad went to the pub every night. It was a ritual made all too easier by the fact it was only two doors away.

"You go ahead with Pascal and Dennis," I said. "Lesley and I will help Mum clean up and I'll get Joanne and Ross into bed. We'll join you in about an hour." Mum would very rarely go to the pub and didn't really drink. Of course, that was perfect for us as she could babysit the children.

Dad was well known in the pub and referred to as "Alec the Pole." He was very proud of his family, so whenever we joined him, he made sure everyone knew who we were. "This is my little baby and her husband Pascal, all the way from Paree. This is Dennis back from America and this is my big baby who is getting married the day after tomorrow." It was always fun and yes, we got to know the regulars. Dad would always throw a pile of bags of potato chips on the table for us to nibble on while we drank.

We always stayed until closing time, although this time Dennis and I headed back a little early. We had an at-home meeting with a social worker the next morning. She was coming over to interview, observe, and report on our interaction with the children.

The next morning she arrived – a nice-looking woman who spent nearly five hours talking with us and even interviewing my parents. It was quite a tense day. We were on edge the whole time, hoping we were saying and doing the right things. We also had no idea how Joanne and Ross would react or what they might say. Dennis had only been home for a few days and they had not seen him for over five months.

How did it go? We had no idea. The social worker showed no emotion, nor did she react to anything we had to say. We were not certain whether she observed anything negative, or positive for that matter, that was relevant to the case to report. We were under so much pressure. All our plans to go to America depended on this interview.

When Dennis opened the door to show her out, it was snowing. "Wow," he said, opening the door wider so I could see.

"Gosh, it's snowing heavily," I said, then looked at the social worker. "Will you be OK?"

"Yes, it looks like it's just started. I don't have far to go," she said.

We wished her a Merry Christmas and she congratulated us on our wedding. Without giving us a clue as to what she was thinking, she was gone. We really didn't want to spend the time analyzing everything. What happened and what was said was done. After all, we were getting married tomorrow, so we needed to focus on the joy of that.

Back inside, Dad had some champagne, and Joanne and Ross were watching television. Dad, always ready to make a toast for any reason, raised a glass. "Let's toast to you getting married tomorrow and to a wonderful future together. What happened today will all work out, you'll see," he said. "Let's celebrate the good things in life, and your love for each other. Cheers!"

I looked up at Dennis, took a deep breath and said, "Yes, it will all work out, and it's snowing, just like the day you asked me out. It feels like a good omen." With that, we drank to all the possibilities of what our future would bring.

Roast Leg of Lamb
with Garlic and Rosemary

This is such a wonderful dish for winter as its time in the oven warms the house and it smells heavenly.

Serves 8

1 leg of lamb (7 pound)
4 garlic cloves
1 tablespoon sea salt
2 tablespoons chopped fresh rosemary

½ teaspoon black pepper
½ cup dry red wine or beef broth
sprig of rosemary, for garnish
salt and freshly ground black pepper

Preheat the oven to 375°F.

Pat the lamb dry and score the fat by making shallow cuts all over with the tip of a small sharp knife. Pound the garlic to a paste with the sea salt and combine with the rosemary and pepper. Place the lamb in a lightly oiled roasting pan, then rub the paste all over it. Let it stand at room temperature for 30 minutes.

Roast the lamb in the middle of the oven until an instant-read thermometer inserted 2 inches into the thickest part of the meat registers 130°F, about 1½ to 1¾ hours. Transfer the lamb to a cutting board and let stand for 15–25 minutes (the temperature will rise to approximately 140°F, which is medium rare).

Add the red wine to the roasting pan and deglaze by boiling over a moderately high heat for 1 minute, stirring and scraping up the brown bits. Strain the sauce and season to taste with salt and pepper.

Carve the lamb into slices and serve with the red wine sauce and a sprig of rosemary.

Roasted Carrots

12 carrots
3 tablespoons olive oil

kosher salt and freshly ground
black pepper

Preheat the oven to 400°F.

Cut the carrots into thick 1-inch chunks.

In a bowl, toss the carrot chunks with the olive oil and season to taste with salt and pepper. Transfer to a sheet pan in one layer and roast in the oven for about 20 minutes, until brown and tender.

Roasted Potatoes

2 pounds yellow-skinned potatoes
2 tablespoons olive oil
1 teaspoon garlic powder

kosher salt and freshly ground
black pepper

Preheat the oven to 425°F.

Peel the potatoes and cut into 2-inch cubes. If time allows, soak the potatoes in cold water for up to an hour (this removes starch and makes for a fluffier potato). Drain and dry the potatoes, then toss them in the olive oil, garlic powder, and salt and pepper to taste.

Roast on a baking sheet for 45 minutes, until brown and tender.

Apple Galette Crumble with Pouring Cream

Simple and rustic, this galette becomes something truly special with the addition of a crumble and heavy pouring cream.

Serves 4

Pastry Shell (Pâte sucrée)

3 cups all-purpose flour
½ cup granulated sugar
½ teaspoon fine salt
1 cup unsalted cold butter, cut
  into pieces
2 large egg yolks

2–4 tablespoons ice water, as needed
1 large egg, lightly beaten, for brushing
coarse sugar, for sprinkling

You will also need:
plastic wrap

In a bowl, blend together the flour, sugar, and salt. Place in a food processor. Add the cold butter pieces and process on pulse mode until the mixture resembles coarse meal.

Add the egg yolks on pulse mode. Add 1 tablespoon of ice water at a time until the mixture forms a dough. Take the dough out of the food processor and flatten into a smooth disk. Cover with plastic wrap and chill in the refrigerator for at least 2 hours.

Let the dough rest at room temperature for 15 minutes before rolling out.

Filling

2 pounds Granny Smith apples,
   peeled, cored, and cut into cubes
½ cup granulated sugar
4 teaspoons all-purpose flour
1 tablespoon fresh lemon juice

¼ teaspoon ground cinnamon
½ cup water

To serve:
pouring cream, to serve

In a large saucepan, combine the apples, granulated sugar, flour, lemon juice, and cinnamon and add the water. Cook over a medium heat until the apples have softened and the water has been absorbed. Take off the heat and let cool.

To assemble the galette

Preheat the oven to 375°F.

Remove the dough from the plastic wrap and, on a lightly floured surface, cut the dough into four pieces. Roll out each piece to about 6 inches square. Divide the apple mixture into four and place each pile in the center of a pastry square. Fold over the sides, leaving an opening in the middle. Brush the pastry with beaten egg. Sprinkle coarse sugar over the pastry and on top of the exposed apples.

Place the galettes on a lightly oiled sheet tray. Bake for about 20 minutes, until the pastry is golden in color.

Serve warm with pouring cream.

Galette aux Pommes de Terre

I couldn't get enough of these when I first had them at my sister's wedding. Creamy sliced russet potatoes tossed with herbs, sour cream, and garlic is yummy and even more so when wrapped in a golden puff pastry packet.

Serves 6

1 packet frozen puff pastry
2 pounds potatoes
1 cup sour cream
1 tablespoon finely chopped fresh
   rosemary
1 tablespoon finely chopped fresh
   chives

1 tablespoon finely minced garlic
1 teaspoon sea salt
cracked fresh black pepper
1 egg yolk
1 tablespoon milk
sea salt and pepper

Preheat the oven to 350°F.

Roll out the puff pastry on a floured board.

Peel the potatoes and slice thinly, using a mandolin. Toss with the sour cream, rosemary, chives, garlic, salt, and pepper to taste.

Divide the puff pastry into two pieces. Place one piece on a sheet pan. Place the potato mixture on top then cover with the other puff pastry sheet. Using a small sharp knife, cut a diamond-shape pattern on top.

Beat the egg yolk and milk together to make an egg wash. Brush over the top of the pastry and sprinkle with sea salt and pepper to taste. Transfer to the oven and bake for 45 minutes, rotating the pan a few times to ensure even browning.

Cool and cut into rectangular slices. Wrap half the slice with parchment paper to serve or, if preferred, place on a plate and eat with a fork.

CHAPTER FIFTEEN
Wedding Bells

We woke up early on our wedding day to get ready for our morning ceremony and luncheon reception. Overnight, a thick blanket of snow had fallen, making everything look magical. We could not have asked for a more picture-perfect day.

Dennis and I were still at my mum and dad's house, adhering to her superstitions that we didn't see each other before the wedding. This was a little hard, as we only had one bathroom for eight people! The house was in absolute wedding chaos, yet Dennis and I were able to dodge one another brilliantly. Everyone would be gathering at the registry office in Broadmead, just off Bristol city center, for the eleven o'clock ceremony.

Dennis was taking the MG and would be driving with his best man, Rich. The two had known each other since they were five. They were like brothers and were always together. If you saw Dennis, Rich wasn't far behind and vice versa. They were the best of buddies, who got into mischief together and had many adventures at a place called "the rocks." Strangely enough, Dennis never took me there and instinctively, I never pressed it. The key to a happy relationship, my mum always told me, was that we all need to keep some things private. The two were so close they had bought a house together, the one on Cat's Ash Lane around the corner from Blostin's where Dennis still lived.

When Rich arrived at the house, Mum gave him his boutonnière and reminded him not to be late getting to the registry office with Dennis. Lesley and Pascal had already left so they could greet guests, and then it was time for me to go.

"I'm ready!" I announced.

Mum looked at me with what I thought might be tears in her eyes. "You look lovely, Paul," she said.

Dad chimed in. "Your mum is right. Not bad. Dennis is a lucky man." In true English tradition, I knew the understatement meant *You look amazing, and we love you so much.* I gave them both a kiss, leaving a lipstick mark on their cheeks. It was the same red Max Factor lipstick Dennis had loved on our first date.

I had decided to wear a simple long-sleeved gray dress belted at the waist, with a deep V-back and trimmed in the front with gray velvet finished with a velvet bow. My hat was gray with a short light pink veil over my eyes. The shoes were gray high heels, and I had a fake fur wrap just in case it got cold, which of course it would. The snow was fresh and would stay looking powdery and beautiful all day.

I know what you are thinking. Here I am, a girl who really loves a party, and yet I didn't go all in for the "big" wedding. We certainly could easily have had a large wedding with all the trimmings, what with my mum being one of sixteen children and the fact that I had fifty-three first cousins! But instead, we decided to keep it to twenty-five guests for many reasons, one of which was that this was the second time around for me. I realized that all that hoopla doesn't mean you will have a happy marriage. We were also squeezing the wedding into the very short window of time Dennis was able to be in England. And, of course, the wedding was quite off season.

Like everything else we had done up to the wedding, Dennis and I made decisions quickly and carried through with them, rarely, if ever, doubting them.

Dad drove Mum, the children, and me to the registry office. I was feeling slightly nervous and had butterflies of excitement in my stomach. Joanne and Ross were sitting on either side of me in the back seat. They looked as cute as buttons. Joanne wore a green floral long-sleeved collared dress, a fur hat with fur bobbles, and a fur hand muff. She loved to dress up and I could tell she was feeling good about herself. On the other hand, Ross, who never wanted to draw attention to himself, humored me and wore terracotta corduroy long trousers and jacket with a matching checkered shirt and reddish-brown shoes. They both sat there quietly, looking out the windows.

Looking at them, I sighed, once again filled with love and gratitude for them. We might not even be here today if they were different people and had reacted badly to all that had happened. They went through my marriage breakup, changed schools and homes, and put up with my odd work hours with ease. And then I introduced a new man into their lives, and they hardly batted an eyelash.

Before we knew it, we had arrived. The registry office was a seventeenth-century single-story gray stone building with arched stone casement windows, which had originally been a Quaker meeting house. Inside it had high ceilings with dark wooden beams. With its history, beauty, and architecture, the building was the perfect backdrop for a wedding.

We lingered outside, where our friends and families had been waiting for us to arrive. Dennis and Rich had not yet arrived. Much to my surprise, also waiting to see us were some neighbors and friends who were not going to the reception. *How lovely is that*, I thought to myself. The energy was high, and the air was filled with anticipation.

With all the drama of Dennis's parents choosing not to attend, I wasn't sure which of his brothers would come. Our two families had never met, so I had to do some introductions. His brother Steve and wife Leslie were there; Sally-Anne came, who is married to Nick, but he could not come as he had to work. Ian and David did not come. It was great to see dear friends Sandra and Roger as well as Alison and Martin and Pam and Mike, who all told me it was touch and go whether they would make it as the roads were treacherous with all the snow.

The wedding ceremony was set for eleven o'clock. It was now ten minutes past. My mother came up to me and whispered, "Dennis is late. He left so much earlier than us. Where do you think he is? He's not getting second thoughts, do you think?"

I couldn't believe he'd have second thoughts. It was more likely that he was lost. I had done my best to prevent this. The other day Dennis and I had made a dry run past the registry office as he didn't know Bristol that well. But I hadn't considered that Rich would be driving.

Just then, out of the corner of my eye, I saw Dennis. He was running as fast as he could down the side of the building. "There he is, Mum!" She gave a little sigh of relief and I had to smile. Never for a moment did I doubt that he would show up, not after all it took for us to get here.

I hadn't seen him for at least a day, thanks to all of Mum's interventions. He looked extremely handsome, although a little frazzled, dressed in a dark gray pinstripe double-breasted suit, black shoes, light blue shirt, and a blue and burgundy striped tie, accented with a burgundy pocket handkerchief.

He headed straight to me and, still trying to catch his breath, said, "Sorry, Peeps. We got lost. I left Rich to park the car."

I just smiled. "Come on, let's go and get married," I said, taking his arm. He had no time to speak to anyone really, but he did take time to say hello to his sister, Pauline, and her husband Andrew. Yes, he has one sister and her name is Pauline, and I was now about to become Pauline Parry Number Two.

By this time, all our guests had settled inside and we were the last to walk in. There was no music and we headed to an unadorned mahogany desk with two chairs for us to sit on. Our guests sat behind us, including Joanne, Ross, and our best man. After a few minutes, an officiant came and sat opposite us. He was wearing a tie with Snoopy on it. I found this funny and gave out a little laugh. I'm sure it was my nerves working overtime and yet details like that stand out.

I don't remember much about the ceremony except that it was swift. Before we knew it, papers were signed, and we were now husband and wife. We stood up and kissed while our guests gave a round of applause.

Outside, the sun had appeared. The snow had stopped but there was still a nip in the air. I kissed and hugged everyone, including all the extra family members and friends who came to wish us well. The photographer gathered us all to take the necessary photos, including capturing the children giving us our lucky horseshoes.

"OK, let's go!" I shouted out to everyone. Before I knew it, Dennis and I were being showered with confetti. Joanne and Ross loved that and could not get enough confetti to throw at us. We'd find confetti everywhere over the next few days.

We headed down the M4, our first moment alone to speak. "I didn't get a chance to say it, but you look absolutely beautiful, Peeps. I can't believe we're married, and you are now my wife. How does it feel to be Mrs. Parry?" I responded like the blushing bride I now was. "It feels exciting. You too look quite handsome."

The drive into the castle took our breath away. It truly was a fairyland. The lawns and vines were covered with pristine snow.

The courtyard was stunning. The restaurant door was open as Fernando came out and said, "Mr. Bell said you could leave your car here rather than taking it to the parking lot." "Fabulous!" I said, getting out of the car. We were greeted by the service team with trays of Bollinger R.D. champagne.

Mr. Bell came up to us both with open arms. "Congratulations! You both look wonderful. Now I want you to relax and enjoy your lunch. We have everything under control." I gave him a hug and kiss on the cheek and Dennis shook his hand. We were so grateful for all he had done for us to make a castle luncheon possible. "We'll savor every single minute of this day," I assured him.

The fire was lit, throwing a warm glow over the entire room. The table – fittingly, a king table – was set in the center of the room, covered in a white cloth and adorned with a few vases of flowers placed down the center. Each place setting only had the charger, napkin, water glass, and the wine glass and flatware for the first course. The staff would set the appropriate flatware and glasses as each course was served.

The pianist, Tony, was playing the grand piano on the raised center window cove. He blew us a kiss as we walked in the dining room. "This is absolutely perfect," I said, looking at Dennis, who was also beaming.

"It looks lovely, Peeps, just like you." With that, he kissed me again, then we joined everyone in the reception area.

The lunch was perfectly amazing as we dined over the next three hours. We began with a brothy leek and potato soup, quite perfect for this cold weather. Our next plate was filled with a beautiful gravlax that was cured at the castle and served with crispy capers. Dennis was very fond of mushrooms so chef stuffed a pork loin with wild mushrooms, herbs, and shallot, with a crispy skin laced with the pork juices.

The children weren't too fond of the food, but they ate what they wanted. We allowed them to go and play with Eva and Ryan as we got into the third course as they were getting a bit fidgety. We finished with a butterscotch pudding layered with caramel.

Nothing was too planned for the afternoon. Our first dance was to Crystal Gayle's song, "Don't It Make My Brown Eyes Blue." My dad made a toast and in true "Dad fashion" ended up getting choked on his words. The best man made his speech, and Andrew, the husband of Pauline Number One, gave a toast on behalf of the Parry family. It was all emotional, with happy tears all around.

We cut the traditional wedding cake – the fruitcake that I had started months ago. I was keeping my fingers crossed that it would be lovely and moist. I sighed with relief as we cut into it – it was. We all continued to dance until it was time to retire into the library for coffee, port, brandy, and, of course, the famous fudge the castle made. Dennis gave the final toast of the day.

"My wife and I," he began, with a little laugh as he sent me a loving look, "would like to thank you from the bottom of our hearts for being with us today, especially braving the snow. Those of you who are here are near and dear to us both and sharing this special day will be a beautiful memory forever.

"It's been quite a wonderful and eventful journey," he continued. He paused and looked over at me again. "Not only did I fall in love with Pauline, but with Joanne and Ross. I cannot believe how lucky I am to have such an amazing package deal." Everyone laughed. "In all seriousness, thank you again for being here." Turning to my parents, he said, "Alec and Joan, I love your daughter so very much and will always take good care of her. Thank you for embracing me into the family. Again, thank you for being here. It means so much for the two of us to share our special day. So, cheers and Merry Christmas to one and all!"

It took us an hour or more to say our farewells as we walked around the room for more intimate conversations with our guests.

As I glanced around the library, everyone seemed content with each other, sipping coffee, wine, water, port, or whatever, which gave me such a warm and fuzzy feeling. I could not have asked for the day to be lovelier.

We finally got to sit with Pauline and Andrew for our last drink of the afternoon. Dennis got on famously with his sister and I understood why. As soon as I met her, I immediately fell in love. Her sense of humor, perspective on life, and joie de vivre always had us laughing. Her husband Andrew, an accomplished screenwriter, is a larger-than-life character who is very theatrical in expressing life experiences. He is one of the best storytellers and, like his wife, outrageously fun to be with. They had been married about ten years and were living in Cornwall with their three lovely children.

"Not to put a damper on the festivities," Andrew opened the conversation, "I want to talk about the elephant in the room. Otherwise known as Mr. and Mrs. Parry."

We were truly sorry they chose not to attend, but, as Andrew pointed out, "They are a breed of their own. Lovely people who sometimes can be judgmental. I know Mrs. Parry desperately wanted to be here, but she had to stand by Mr. Parry. It's the era they came from. They will come round, sooner rather than later, and will regret not having been here.

"In the meantime, we love you, so let's make a toast. To the family that are here to share this joyous occasion. May you have a long and happy life together," he said, in true Andrew fashion.

It finally came time to leave. I wrapped my fur around my neck as I walked out in the night air. Someone had written "Just Married" on the back window and there were half a dozen cans tied on the back bumper with string. We looked at the children, who were giggling with their hands on their mouths. Yes, they must have been part of the big secret of doing this. *What fun!* we both thought, and laughed.

I gave my parents a big kiss and turned to Joanne and Ross. "Now, you need to be good for Grandma and Dziadek. We'll be home on Christmas Eve. Remember, Father Christmas comes that night for all the well-behaved children," I said, giving them a hug and a kiss. Dennis followed behind me, doing the same. They weren't upset we were leaving and, like everyone else, were just waiting to give us a fond farewell.

We got into the car, waving goodbye out the windows. We could hear the clanking of the cans as we drove off and the sounds of the "goodbyes" in the distance.

As the car turned the corner and we were out of sight, Dennis stopped the car, turned to me, and said, "I love you," and then sealed it with a kiss. With that, he put the car into gear and we were off, taking the country lanes to the Royal Crescent Hotel in Bath, where Dennis had reserved the Sir Percy Blakeney Suite for our two-night honeymoon. The Royal Crescent is a spectacular row of Georgian terraced houses laid out in a perfect curve. We stopped the car right outside the hotel entrance at No 16.

Taking our bags, we locked the car and walked inside the hotel. We left the car there, not caring that "Just Married" was written on the window or cans were tied to the bumper. They stayed there until we returned to the car two days later to drive back home.

Leek and Potato Soup

This soup is an elegant first course, or if you want to serve it with a salad and a loaf of crunchy bread, it's perfect for a snowy day.

Serves 4

1 pound leeks, white parts only,
    cleaned
3 tablespoons unsalted butter
2 celery stalks, diced
1 pound white onions, peeled
    and diced

1 pound yellow potatoes, peeled
    and diced
6 cups vegetable stock
½ teaspoon white pepper
kosher salt
1 tablespoon snipped chives,
    for garnish

Chop the leeks into small pieces.

Melt the butter in a large saucepan over medium heat. Add the leeks, celery, onions, and a heavy pinch of salt and sweat for 5 minutes. Decrease the heat to medium-low and cook for about 25 minutes, stirring occasionally, until the leeks are tender.

Add the potatoes, vegetable stock, and pepper. Increase the heat to medium-high and bring to a boil. Reduce the heat to low, cover, and gently simmer for about 30 minutes, until the potatoes are soft.

Turn off the heat and puree the mixture in a blender until smooth. Serve immediately in soup bowls, sprinkled with chives.

Salmon Gravlax Carpaccio

This is an elegant recipe that celebrates a beautiful ingredient – smoked Scottish center-cut salmon served with crispy capers, red onion, and fresh dill, with an extra virgin olive oil dressing.

Serves 2

Dressing

¼ cup good extra virgin olive oil
1 garlic clove, finely chopped
1 tablespoon fresh lemon juice

1 teaspoon grainy Dijon mustard
1 small red onion, halved lengthwise
and thinly sliced into half moons

Combine all the dressing ingredients in a bowl and whisk until well combined.

Crispy Capers

2 tablespoons drained capers
1 teaspoon all-purpose flour

2 tablespoons extra virgin olive oil

In a bowl, toss the drained capers in the flour until evenly coated. Heat the olive oil in a small nonstick skillet over medium heat. When the skillet is hot, add the capers and cook for about 3 minutes, until golden brown and crisp. Transfer the capers to a plate lined with a paper towel and let cool.

For the Salmon

8 ounces center-cut Scottish smoked
  salmon, thinly sliced
1 tablespoon loosely chopped fresh dill
freshly cracked black pepper,
  for garnish

2 ounces crème fraîche
grissini breadsticks
½ lemon, covered with cheesecloth

Line a salad plate with the salmon in a single layer of slices. Spoon
the dressing evenly over the salmon. Top with crispy capers and
finish with chopped fresh dill, cracked black pepper, and blobs of
crème fraîche. Serve with grissini breadsticks and the half lemon.

Pork Roulade with Mushrooms

One of my favorites with its elegant presentation, this pork tenderloin is butterflied and stuffed with an herb mushroom mixture and served with a sherry au jus sauce.

Serves 6

7 tablespoons extra virgin olive oil

1 pound mushrooms, such as cremini, shiitake, and oyster, roughly chopped

1 small head of garlic, minced

½ cup finely chopped fresh parsley

1 tablespoon finely chopped fresh thyme, plus 2 sprigs

1 tablespoon finely chopped fresh rosemary, plus 1 sprig

1 center-cut boneless pork loin (3–4 pounds)

1 cup dry sherry

1 cup chicken broth

1 tablespoon unsalted butter

kosher salt and freshly ground pepper

6 sprigs thyme, for garnish

You will also need:

butcher's string

aluminum foil

Preheat the oven to 350°F.

Heat 1 tablespoon of the olive oil in a large nonstick skillet over medium-high heat. Add the mushrooms and cook for about 2 minutes, undisturbed, until they start browning. Stir and continue cooking for 4–5 minutes, stirring occasionally, until tender. Push the mushrooms to one side of the skillet and add another 1 tablespoon of olive oil and the garlic to the other side. Cook for about 30 seconds, stirring occasionally, until softened. Stir the garlic into the mushrooms, season to taste with salt and pepper, and let cool.

In a small bowl, combine the chopped parsley, thyme, and rosemary with 3 tablespoons of the olive oil and a pinch each of salt and pepper. Set aside.

Butterfly the pork by positioning your knife about one-third of the way up the length of the pork loin, with your knife parallel to the cutting board. Begin cutting into the pork, pulling the meat away with your other hand so that it opens up into a flat, evenly thick piece. Season the pork with salt and pepper to taste, spread the herb oil over the top, and top with the mushrooms. Reroll the pork into a log and tie at 1-inch intervals using butcher's string. Season to taste with salt and pepper.

Set a rack in a large roasting pan. Heat the remaining 2 tablespoons of olive oil in a large skillet over medium-high heat. Add the pork, fat side down, and cook for about 3 minutes, until browned. Continue to cook, turning, for a further 1–2 minutes, until browned all over. Transfer the pork seam side down to the rack in the pan. Roast on the lower rack in the oven until a thermometer inserted into the thickest part of the meat (not the filling) registers 135°F, 1 hour to 1 hour 15 minutes. Remove the pork to a cutting board, tent with foil, and let it rest for 30 minutes.

In the meantime, skim off any excess fat from the juices in the roasting pan and add the sherry. Place the pan across two burners over medium-high heat. Add the thyme and rosemary sprigs and cook for 1 minute, scraping up any browned bits with a wooden spoon and stirring, until the liquid is reduced by about half. Strain the sauce through a fine mesh sieve. Pour into a small saucepan, add the chicken broth, and bring to a boil. Lower the heat to a simmer and cook for 4–5 minutes, until slightly reduced. Stir in the butter and season to taste with salt.

Remove the twine from the pork and cut the pork into 1-inch thick slices. Serve with the sauce, garnished with fresh thyme sprigs.

Butterscotch Pudding
with Salted Caramel

Butterscotch pudding is quite overlooked as a fancy dessert. But it easily goes to the next level with a layer of salted caramel, topped with a whipped cream rosette and served with rolled wafers.

Serves 6

Butterscotch Custard

3 tablespoons salted butter

1 cup brown sugar

¼ cup cornstarch

1 cup heavy cream

2 cups whole milk

3 egg yolks

2 teaspoons pure vanilla extract

Melt the butter in a heavy-bottomed saucepan over medium heat. Add the sugar and keep stirring until the sugar and butter are completely melted. Stir in the cornstarch. Add the heavy cream and whole milk, bring to a slow rolling boil, and let thicken. Continue to cook, stirring, until the mixture coats the back of the spoon.

Meanwhile, place the egg yolks in a small bowl. Temper the egg yolks by spooning a small amount of the hot milk into the bowl. Use a whisk and keep stirring. Pour the mixture back into the pot. Bring back to a boil for 1 minute. Add the vanilla extract. Place the custard in 6 small glasses and let it cool in the refrigerator.

Salted Caramel

1 cup sugar
½ cup unsalted butter
½ cup heavy cream
¼ teaspoon sea salt (plus more
  for the top of the caramel)

To serve:
1 cup whipped cream
Rolled wafers, such as Pepperidge
  Farm or Pirouline, for garnish

Heat the sugar in a medium saucepan over medium heat, stirring constantly. The sugar will begin to form clumps and will turn an amber color. Keep stirring. Watch carefully as the sugar can easily burn. Once the sugar is completely melted, use a whisk to stir the butter into the sugar. Drizzle the heavy cream into the mixture and stir. Let it boil for 1 minute, stirring occasionally. Remove from the heat and stir in the sea salt.

Let the caramel cool slightly and then pour it over the top of the custard. Sprinkle a little sea salt over the caramel, then add a rosette of whipped cream and a rolled wafer.

Wedding Fruitcake

Fruitcake is a traditional wedding cake for the royal family in England, making it a popular choice for many Brits. It's a bit of an undertaking to age the cake so get ready to start it three months before you want to serve it. Made with glacé cherries, candied peel, golden and black raisins, and ground almonds, covered with marzipan and royal icing and decorated with marzipan holly and berries, it's a cause for celebration.

Serves 12

4 cups golden and black raisins

10 fluid ounces brewed strong
  cold black tea

8 ounces unsalted butter, slightly
  softened

8 ounces brown sugar

5 eggs, beaten one at a time

2 cups all-purpose flour

2 tablespoons molasses

3 ounces brandy

½ teaspoon ground nutmeg

2 teaspoons freshly squeezed
  lemon juice

1 teaspoon baking powder

4 ounces ground almonds

4 ounces glacé cherries, chopped

4 ounces candied peel, chopped

You will also need:

plastic wrap

cheesecloth, to wrap the cake

3 fluid ounces brandy, to soak
  the cheesecloth in

The day before baking, place the black and golden raisins in a large bowl, add the cold tea, and stir well. Cover and let stand overnight.

Preheat the oven to 325°F. Line an 8-inch round cake pan with parchment paper.

Place the butter and sugar in a large mixer bowl. Whisk until pale, smooth, and creamy. Beat 1 egg into the creamed butter, then beat in ¼ cup of flour. Repeat until all the eggs and flour are used up. Add the molasses, brandy, nutmeg, and lemon juice to the cake mixture, and stir gently using a spatula. Stir in the baking powder.

Drain the dried fruits and place them in a bowl along with the ground almonds, glacé cherries, and candied peel. Stir well, then add to the cake mixture, stirring gently until all the fruits are incorporated into the mixture. Spoon the mixture into the prepared cake pan, level the cake mixture, then put a slight dip in the center of the mixture so that, when cooked, it has a flat top rather than a domed top.

To age the cake, soak cheesecloth in brandy and wrap the cake. Then cover the cake in plastic wrap and store in a cool, dark place. Resoak the cheesecloth once a week, every week for up to 3 months.

A week before you are ready to serve the cake, wrap it in marzipan, ready-made from most large grocery stores. Let that dry for 2 days, then cover with royal icing. Decorate with festive ribbon, silver bells, or marzipan holly and berries.

CHAPTER SIXTEEN
The Holidays

The festive ribbons and cans that were still on the back of our car made a loud clanging sound as we drove into my parents' driveway. They had been doing that all the way back from Bath. We hadn't removed them, or the "Just Married" sign that the children had painted on the car two days before. We were ecstatic about being married and wanted to tell the world. And, if truth be told, we'd been a little busy celebrating our honeymoon.

Before we could even get out of the car, Joanne and Ross came running out of the house to greet us. I picked up Ross and Dennis picked up Joanne. "Hello, my darlings," I cried out as I smothered Ross with kisses and he wriggled happily in my arms. "Have you missed us?" They didn't answer, but the fact that they had their arms wrapped around our necks was answer enough. We left the bags for later and went inside, the children still hanging on to us as if we'd been away for years.

The house was cozy and warm with a fire crackling away and all the Christmas decorations up. We found everyone in the kitchen, as always, gathered around the table. Lesley and Pascal were making a cup of tea. Dad was preparing a turkey, the Bigos was cooking on the stove top, and the countertops were piled high with fresh fruit, nuts, chocolate, and various sausages and meats Dad had bought that day – another excursion to the butcher shop with the children, and this time accompanied by Lesley and Pascal.

Mum was anxious to hear all the details. "What was the hotel like?" she asked as she handed Dennis and me cups of hot tea.

"It was fabulous," we said at the same time. Dennis continued, "We had a huge three-room suite. The bathroom must have been as big as this kitchen," gesturing with a sweep of his arm. He was always focused on the architectural details, naturally, whereas my memories were about the food, the service, and how wonderful it all made us feel. "There was champagne and a fruit and cheese platter when we arrived. They'd lit the fire and even pulled back the bed covers so all we had to do was slip into bed and cover up." I had taken keen note of all this while we were there, assessing what I might be able to incorporate into the castle's hospitality efforts.

"It was so romantic. Quite perfect for newlyweds, or anyone else for that matter who was in the mood for love," I said, smiling. One of my favorite details that the staff had considered was how we'd feel the moment we walked in. When we arrived in the late afternoon, the curtains on the floor-to-ceiling windows were open. The view was of manicured lawns covered with fresh snow, and in the distance the lights of the city glowed.

Mum listened intently to my description of the hotel while everyone else buzzed around the table, getting ready for Christmas dinner. Pascal was organizing the champagne while Ross and Joanne helped get the glasses out. Dad was still working on his dinner specials and Lesley was getting another cup of tea. Christmas carols played on the radio in the background. *Life is good*, I thought. No wonder I feel comfortable in this world of hospitality. I was brought up with people who cared about creating a celebration around all the big and small moments in life.

They cared about one another's comforts, joys, and happiness. This was ingrained in me.

"What about the food?" Mum asked.

"We only ventured out for lunch yesterday," I answered. "We hadn't eaten since the wedding and we were starving. The hotel concierge told us about this cute pizza place that made pizza in a wood-burning oven. I hadn't heard of that, so we had to try it. It was a short walk from the hotel."

The pizza place was a do-it-yourself concept. It might have been all the rage in London but it was only just starting to catch on in rural and destination areas such as Bath. All they served was pizza and the customer could choose the toppings. They offered just that and a very simple green salad with Parmesan and olive oil dressing – nothing more, nothing less. As for wine, they only had two choices – an Italian red or an Italian white.

"Now, isn't that a brilliant concept? A great product and price. No frills," I said to everyone. The pizza had been delicious and as we were eating it, Dennis and I couldn't help but analyze the business model – they kept their inventory and staff to a minimum so they could concentrate on the best-quality food. As I was once again mulling that over, thinking about how I could incorporate this into the hotel's recent refresh, a glass of champagne was put in my hand. "Oh, lovely!" Who doesn't love some champagne? Pascal gave Joanne and Ross a flute with orange juice and a tiny splash of champagne. They were feeling quite grown-up, sitting around the table with us all.

"Time for a toast!" Dad announced, holding up his glass. We all held up our glasses and waited for Dad to begin. "Welcome to the family, Dennis. Now that you are part of it, there is something you need to know about Pauline, my big bambino." I held my breath, not sure what he was going to say. "She is a hard worker but can be a handful at times. You need to make sure you keep her in line as she sometimes has too much to say." There was laughter all around, as we all understood his cheeky sense of humor. "Aww, thanks, Dad," I said, going along with it.

"But seriously," he continued, matching his tone to his words. "Your Mum and I wish you a long and happy life. Remember, if you've got your health, you have everything, so always take care of yourselves. And to my little bambini," he said, looking at Joanne and Ross, "be good and take care of your Mum and Dennis." With that, he finished with his usual line, *Salute per tutta la nostra vita.* Translated, this means "Health throughout our lives," and true to his big-hearted nature, he said it with tears in his eyes.

Christmas Day was wonderful. Joanne and Ross had us up early as they were unbelievably excited to see if Father Christmas had left them any gifts. Yes, they still believed. All the family came over for an early Christmas dinner. Lesley and I set the table, which included the Christmas crackers. As usual, Lesley and Pascal brought the wine. Because Mum and Angela didn't eat poultry, we roasted a sirloin beef joint in addition to the turkey. For dessert, we had all the traditional fare – Christmas cake, Christmas pudding, brandy butter, mince pies, whipped cream, and trifle.

The conversation centered around our wedding as we all relived the day, each of us bringing different stories and memories. Of course, the big topic of conversation was our plans to emigrate to America.

"When will you know if you can go?" Angela asked.

"When we get sole custody of the children, Dennis can get all the paperwork in place for us all," I answered. "It takes a bit longer to get the paperwork together as a family and not just as an individual."

We all agreed the uncertainty of the situation was nerve-racking. It put many details of our lives on hold as we sorted it all out. Of course, there was a Plan B. We could remain in England and rethink everything, from our careers to where we would live and so much more. This would not have been bad, but our hearts were set on our new venture and we were only focusing on our move to America, taking everything one step at a time.

In true Kaniecki fashion, Angela made another toast. "Here's to a bright future and wishing you nothing but success in moving forward with your life in America." Dennis and I looked at each other with a sigh. *Yes.*

We were glad Joanne and Ross were not around during this conversation as we still hadn't said anything to them. *Why would we?* I reasoned. *Until all the paperwork is in place, we're not certain we'll be going.*

The next day, Lesley and Pascal left to travel back to France and Joanne and Ross were picked up by their dad to spend the New Year with him. As Dennis and I were still officially on our honeymoon and I wasn't due back to work until the new year, we stayed with Mum and Dad. With everyone gone, it was wonderful to have this quality time with them. I cooked for us all, giving Mum a rest from the kitchen. We would join Dad in the pub on his nightly jaunts and even Mum came with us a couple of times. I felt I was being the "perfect wife" as I carried out my daily shopping and preparation of meals.

Dennis had never really seen me in this role as we'd never lived together. He would always visit and leave, or we would be out on dates. I suppose this short interlude with my parents was the reality of how our life would be moving forward, and we would be working, and oh, that's right ... we'd have two children to take care of. I smiled to myself at the thought. *We'll balance it all out between us, I'm certain.*

Sunday dinner was coming up and I thought of making Dennis a roasted goose. He absolutely loved it, but goose wasn't readily available. However, Mum's local butcher said he could get one for me. "Mum, I got the goose. Let's surprise Dennis and Dad and cook that for our late Sunday roast tomorrow. I'll win his heart all over again." Then, remembering that my mum couldn't eat it, I quickly added, "I'll be sure and cook something special for you."

"No, don't bother. There'll be enough for me to eat without it," she said. And she was right.

While Dennis and Dad were at the pub, we began getting the feast ready. Mum and I had already picked the brussels sprouts from the frosted stalks in the garden. We had potatoes and runner beans from the summer harvest. And we had already prepped the traditional stuffing, to which we added apples from the garden that were ripening on top of the kitchen cabinets.

I pierced the goose skin all over with a sharp skewer so the excess fat would release while cooking. This would make the skin nice and crispy and hopefully keep the breast a juicy light pink inside. All that extra fat would be perfect to roast the potatoes. I had simply cut those in half so when cooked they would be crunchy on the outside and soft in the middle. I'd make the gravy from the rest of the juices and fat and add the water from the vegetables we were cooking to finish the gravy, thickened with a little cornstarch. It was all looking incredibly delicious.

We heard the chatter as Dad and Dennis came through the front door. "We are starving," Dad said, clapping his hands together dramatically to get them warm.

"Whatever we're having, it smells delicious," Dennis said.

I just looked at him coyly. "Wait until you see what I have for you! Can you and Dad open the wine while Mum and I finish getting dinner plattered up?"

Everyone was at the dinner table when I entered with the platters. "Goose! I don't believe it!" Dennis exclaimed in complete surprise. He came over and gave me a big kiss.

"That's my girl," my dad said. "She knows how to put on a feast." As usual, Dad started with a toast and once again we were enjoying our favorite pastime – food, wine, and conversation around the dining table.

I had originally planned to serve all the leftover desserts from Christmas but decided to make one of Dennis's favorites. I thought the occasion called for something special... and lighter, as the main meal was rich. I made a pavlova with whipped heavy cream topped with mandarins and sliced pears. It was a winner, with Dad making another toast "to the chef," which Dennis and Mum joined in. I was completely satisfied, in both my heart and my tummy.

Things were blissful, except that Dennis was starting to feel terrible about what had happened with his parents over the wedding. I personally didn't care. I was still infuriated that they could be so unreasonable and cruel to their son. It wasn't clear if they were trying to hurt me, but they were certainly hurting Dennis.

One morning during our Christmas holiday, after talking to Mum and Dad about it, and asking Dennis what he thought, I called the Parrys and invited them over for dinner. For me, it's hard to hold a grudge when you are having an excellent meal together. I was hoping this was the same for them. Perhaps it would mend the situation and possibly close the gap between us.

Mr. Parry answered the phone. "Hello, this is Pauline, Dennis's wife," I said. I didn't want him to think it was his daughter, the other Pauline. There was silence. I took a deep breath and continued. "My parents and I would like to invite you and Mrs. Parry for dinner with us all before Dennis goes back to America. Would you come?"

There was a pause, then he said, "You need to speak to Mrs. Parry."

"Before you pass me over to her," I continued, not wanting to let go of this opportunity to talk to him, "if she says yes, can I assume you would also join us?" He mumbled something, I'm not sure what, and before I knew it, Mrs. Parry was on the phone.

I asked her the same question and she immediately said, "Yes, that would be wonderful." I arranged to have Dennis pick them up at 5:30 p.m. the next day. "We'll be ready," she responded. I could hear in her voice that she was happy and resolved to make the situation right.

"Does 'we' mean Mr. Parry will come too?"

"Yes, he will," she said in a defiant tone of voice that made me smile.

The next evening, Dennis picked his parents up and I waited at the door as they walked from the car. I kissed them both hello and was completely surprised to find no sense of irritation on their part. It was as if nothing had happened. Clearly, they had come to a place of acceptance over the wedding, and perhaps a little bit of remorse over having missed it? I couldn't be sure right away.

We talked about everything but the wedding. Mum and Dad were great at putting everyone at ease. We chatted about music, football, the food, and the weather. It wasn't until Dad took Dennis and Mr. Parry into the lounge to have a brandy that the floodgates opened for Mrs. Parry.

"I have been so upset about this whole situation," Mrs. Parry blurted out as soon as she was alone with Mum and me. "I know you shouldn't have favorites with your children, but Dennis is my favorite and not being at his wedding broke my heart."

Apparently, they had been listening to gossip – always a mistake in my book – and thought Dennis was making a bad choice with me. "We were worried that as a divorcee with two children, you might be taking our son to the cleaners. Mr. Parry had made up his mind about you and it was something I couldn't change. I had to stand by his side, right or wrong," she continued. I had to laugh at the thought of me as a gold digger.

"Please forgive us," she said. "I was with you in spirit on your wedding day and cried most of that day. I know we have made a huge mistake and I hope you will forgive us." She looked at me and I could tell she was so sad still. My heart ached as a mother myself for what she was going through. She'd never be able to go back in time and see her son get married, but at least she and her husband were here now, ready to begin to repair a love that was so obviously strong.

"Of course I will," I said, holding back tears… I was my father's daughter, after all! "We can't turn back the clock, but we can move forward. Dennis will be extremely happy that you and Mr. Parry will be in our lives."

I didn't expect the evening to go like that at all but was very happy it did. The Parrys stayed for another couple of hours. We even all danced in the lounge. Mr. Parry never spoke about the situation whatsoever, even when we were driving them home at two o'clock in the morning. We kissed them good night and said we'd see them next week before Dennis had to leave for America.

Dennis and I walked his parents to the door of their house and made sure they were safely inside. As we got back in the car, we looked at each other and laughed. It was the laughter that came with relief. A stressful situation had been defused, and fairly easily. We had to laugh at the absurdity of it all. It was heartbreaking that they weren't at the wedding, but, like most times in life, one can laugh or cry. We chose to laugh.

Pizza with Parmesan Arugula Salad

Culinary trends don't always move fast, but on our honeymoon in Bath the concept of make-your-own pizza had arrived. The hotel concierge suggested it and we loved the idea, new to us at the time! This is one that we chose – crispy pizza dough topped with mozzarella, tomato, olives, basil, and red onions, finished with a swirl of olive oil and sprinkled with coarse sea salt, served with arugula dusted with Parmesan.

Makes one 12-inch pizza

Pizza Crust

1 ¼ ounce packet active dry yeast

1 teaspoon white sugar

1 cup warm water (110°F)

2½ cups bread flour

1 teaspoon kosher salt

2 tablespoons olive oil

Toppings *– enough for a 12-inch pizza*

mozzarella cheese

thinly sliced vine-ripened tomatoes

halved black olives

thinly sliced red onion

torn basil leaves

extra virgin olive oil

coarse sea salt

Arugula Salad

arugula

extra virgin olive oil

finely grated Parmesan

coarse sea salt and cracked black pepper

Place a pizza stone on a rack in the oven. Preheat the oven to 450°F.

In a medium bowl, dissolve the yeast and sugar in the warm water. Let stand for about 10 minutes, until creamy. Stir in the flour, salt, and oil and beat until smooth. Let rest for 5 minutes.

Turn the dough out onto a lightly floured surface and pat or roll it into a round. Transfer the crust to a lightly greased baker's peel. Place the mozzarella cheese on the crust and top with the sliced tomatoes, halved olives, sliced red onion, and basil leaves.

Place the pizza on the stone in the oven and cook for about 15 minutes, until the dough is crisp around the edges and at the bottom. Remove from the oven. Drizzle extra virgin olive oil over the top and sprinkle with coarse sea salt. Serve with arugula lightly dressed with extra virgin olive oil, dusted with Parmesan and salt and pepper to taste.

Roast Goose with Brussels Sprouts, Half Potatoes, Green Beans, and Gravy

The first meal I made for Dennis as a newly married woman was this show stopper! You can get goose from a specialty market or a butcher, although you might have to pre-order it.

Serves 6

1 goose, about 8 pounds
1 lemon, cut in half
1 head of garlic cloves
1 yellow onion, peeled and chopped
1 tablespoon flour

½ cup Madeira wine
1 cup chicken broth
1 teaspoon dried thyme
kosher salt and pepper

Preheat the oven to 325°F.

Remove the giblets, neck, and wing tips to use for making gravy. Prick the goose skin all over with a needle. The technique is to stick the skin from an angle so you are not piercing the meat of the goose, just the skin. Doing this will allow the fat somewhere to go and allow the skin to get crispy.

Rub the goose all over with the lemon halves, then place them inside the goose. Sprinkle with salt liberally, inside and out. Slice the top off the head of garlic and place it inside the goose. Place the goose, breast side up, on a rack in a roasting pan. Place in the oven and cook for about 1 hour 15 minutes, until golden and crispy.

Meanwhile, start cooking the gravy. Chop the giblets, neck, and wing tips and brown them in a medium saucepan. Sprinkle with salt. Add the chopped onion and stir to combine. When the onion gets a little brown, sprinkle the flour in the pan and cook over medium heat, stirring often, until it smells nutty, about 5–10 minutes. Turn the heat up to high and add the Madeira. Let it boil for a minute then add the chicken broth and stir to combine. Add the dried thyme, reduce the heat to a bare simmer, and cook for about 20 minutes, until thickened.

Remove the goose from the oven – the internal temperature should be approximately 170°F – and let it rest. Remove the garlic cloves from the husk and add to the gravy. Strain the gravy through a fine mesh sieve. Place the goose on a wooden board and carve. Serve with the gravy, butter poached brussels sprouts, green beans, and potatoes roasted in the goose fat.

Pear and Mandarin Pavlova

I made this dessert for a special dinner of roast goose with my family after Dennis and I were married. The soft-center crispy meringue is topped with whipped cream and fresh sliced pears, mandarins, and raspberries (frozen from the summer harvest), with mint garnish. It's refreshing after a roast dinner.

Serves 6

Meringue

6 large egg whites, room temperature
1½ cups granulated sugar
½ teaspoon lemon juice

½ teaspoon vanilla extract
2 teaspoons cornstarch

Cream

1½ cups heavy whipping cream

2 tablespoons granulated sugar

Whip together in a mixing bowl for 2–3 minutes, until spreadable.

Fruit

4 cups thin sliced pears, mandarins,
* and raspberries*

fresh mint sprigs, for garnish

Preheat the oven to 225°F.
    Line a large baking sheet with parchment paper.

Using a mixer, beat the egg whites on high for about 1 minute, until soft peaks form. Gradually beat in the sugar and beat for about 10 minutes, until stiff peaks form. The mixture will be smooth and glossy.

Using a spatula, quickly fold in the lemon juice and vanilla extract, then the cornstarch, and mix until well blended.

Pipe the meringue into 3-inch wide nests on the parchment paper. Indent the center with a spoon to allow room for the cream. Bake for 1 hour and 15 minutes, then turn off the oven. Without opening the door, let the meringue stay in the oven for a further 30 minutes. The outside will be crisp to the tap and inside will still be marshmallow soft.

Transfer the parchment to a cookie rack and let the meringues cool to room temperature. Once cool, top them with whipped cream and fruit and garnish with a fresh mint sprig.

CHAPTER SEVENTEEN
Final Decisions

Once again, I was driving Dennis to London Heathrow. The trip had gone by faster than we imagined but it was filled to the brim. We got married, had a honeymoon, albeit a short one of just two days, resolved the issue with Dennis's parents, and even met with the social worker who would be a big part of deciding our fate.

"Hopefully we'll only have to do this one more time," Dennis said as I reached out to put my hand on his. "The next time we will be going as a family." I nodded my head, too worried to jinx what had to happen next by saying anything out loud.

We were getting to be pros at the airport run. We parked the car and got him to the gate and on the plane in record time. As I walked back to the car, though, all my worries set in again.

One week later, I sat in the solicitor's office, wishing Dennis was with me. My solicitor had met with my ex-husband David and his team earlier that day and was filling me in on what to expect.

"I've seen the brief, Pauline, and it won't be pretty. Are you ready?" He told me that David and his team of solicitors were going to paint me in a bad light. They were planning to bring up the fact that I had taken on a job in hospitality (which was still seen as not favorable for a woman), that I had moved the children into an apartment above a restaurant rather than a proper house, and that I worked long, erratic hours. To me, all these things were pluses. I could work and still see the children as much as they needed. I was only a stairwell away from them. Everything in my day was designed around their lives and they were happy and well adjusted.

But still, I hated the fact that this was being used against me. "How unfair is this?" I cried out to my solicitor. I was the injured party, the innocent in all this. He was the one who had had the affair. He was the one who messed our lives up and now he wanted to do it again. I was angry and defiant.

"Anger won't help you," my solicitor said. "I agree with you, but you can't get angry. We'll present your case to the judge. You'll see. It'll be alright."

I nodded. I was happy he felt confident. I stopped feeling sorry for myself and instead began to get myself together, ready to show the judge how much I loved my children. "Got it," I said to him. This was a crucial time in our lives, there was no room for error. Dennis and I had now made up our minds – America was where we wanted to be with the children.

On the way back to the castle, I cleared my mind of the case. There was too much to be done at work that needed my undivided attention. "It will all work out," I said out loud. I was hopeful that it would, but saying it out loud made me start to believe it. I had to.

At the castle, we had all been working like crazy to get the hotel rooms ready for the soft opening in another month. Mr. Bell had suggested that I stay in each room before the opening so I could see if anything might be missing. We wanted to make sure our guests had the ultimate experience. I did that once a week, after my Saturday shifts. I felt like I was living in the lap of luxury. Mr. Bell and Molly had done a superb job in designing each room, giving them all their own special touches as well as ensuring all the essentials to provide our guests with an outstanding stay.

While all the rooms had a common thread of rich, traditional, and majestic overtones, each one had its own personality. Some were rustic, with wood paneling, wooden ceiling beams, and stone walls, while others were more luxe, adorned with stylized wall-papers and heavily draped curtains tied back with rope tassels. Most of them had high four-poster beds draped with puffy duvets and extra-large pillows, perfect to sink your head in as you drifted into sleep. Bathrooms varied but most had black-and-white marble tiles and a freestanding bathtub. And for an added touch of luxury, towels stood at the ready on heated rails.

The castle was L-shaped, with a large grass courtyard in the middle. The restaurant was on one side of the castle, which was on two levels. The seven rooms, accessed by two stairwells, were on the second level, above the restaurant, the commercial kitchen, and the lounge area. When the restaurant was closed, it seemed a little eerie as there was no activity. Obviously when the hotel opened, we would have activity until the restaurant closed at about midnight, and of course the registration desk would be open.

While I was testing the room experience, I was the only person on that side of the castle, which was a little spooky. It was deathly silent as the restaurant was closed. One of my notes for Mr. Bell: Some classical music playing in the rooms when guests enter would be a nice touch.

While the castle was quiet at night, it was buzzing in the day. Over the past month we had been interviewing staff, preparing policies and guidelines. We had also developed menus for afternoon tea and breakfast, and were now working on the lunch menu. It truly was a massive undertaking.

In addition, for our new refreshed look at the castle, Mr. Bell had ordered new uniforms for the staff. For the ladies, this was a terracotta-colored skirt and vest with a white shirt. The men wore the same color vest and shirt but with black trousers and tie. A new reception area, where we would greet guests, had also been built. As we put the elements together for the hotel opening, I was working there often.

Four days before opening, the rooms were fully booked, and the restaurant too was nearly filled to capacity, although we left some tables available in case any guests wanted to dine at the hotel. I was envisioning a grand opening, with Mr. Bell greeting guests and attending to their hospitality needs, and so I was a little shocked when Mr. Bell and Molly approached me as they were leaving the restaurant a week before we opened. "Molly and I have decided to take a trip to the Caribbean next week. I am leaving you and Fernando in charge."

"Of the opening?" I asked. I'm sure I looked stunned. "You won't be here?" I croaked out. With a wave of his hand, he dismissed the notion that leaving me alone in charge of the opening was anything but an everyday occurrence. "You are going to do fine. Everything looks fantastic and after all, Molly and I need to have a little holiday to recharge."

What could I say but, "That's fine, Mr. Bell. How will we reach you if there are any problems?" Again, he pooh-poohed my fear. "I'll leave the name of where we are staying, but please, only get in touch with us if the building is burning down." As he walked away, he laughed and said, "We leave tomorrow. We have no doubt that we leave it all in your capable hands."

Well OK, I thought as I was walking back to the gatehouse, finished with work for the evening. It's not every day someone gives you the opportunity to open a hotel. *And what's one more challenge?* I laughed to myself. Even Mr. Bell had never opened a hotel. He must think it will be easy if he's going on holiday. *Let's hope he's right*, I thought as I kissed the children good night. I got a good night's sleep before opening day.

In the morning, I walked around the castle with Fernando and Sharon, the head housekeeper. We checked everything one more time, finding only a few things that had to be put right. "I think everything looks lovely. I'm so pleased we decided to splurge on flowers. It gives a fresh garden look, giving warmth to the place," I said, looking at Fernando and Sharon. "Ready?" I asked.

"Ready!" they answered.

I felt like we were launching a rocket and said so. We all laughed, and I felt the tension start to melt immediately. No one wants to come into a hotel with a lot of tense staff. "We can do this," we all said, and with that, we went in different directions.

Mr. Bell was right. He had nothing to worry about as he relaxed on a beach somewhere. Did the opening weekend go flawlessly? No, we had our challenges, but as I had already discovered in my first few years in the hospitality industry, we can spin on a dime and find solutions to problems in an instant. There were no fires, so we left Mr. Bell and Molly alone to enjoy their well-deserved break.

Critics are a necessary part of any industry in which the general public is involved and we weren't immune. Thank goodness we didn't know there was a hotel critic there during the opening. We found out later that he had stayed in Room 7, the smallest room we had. It wasn't the most dramatic of rooms – there was not a massive four-poster-bed – but it definitely had a plush coziness.

I happened to be at registration when this gentleman came to check out. "Thank you for your hospitality," he said, placing his key on the counter. "I sincerely hope everything was comfortable for you," I said. "It certainly was. I also had dinner in the tower, it was delicious," he went on to say. I thought back to what the special of the night was – it had been Warm Crab Salad layered with Crispy Phyllo Pastry. In addition, there was Duck Confit with Red Currant Sauce served with lentils and a crispy blanket of pancetta. I had tried it before the dinner service, and it was truly a special meal.

After settling his account, he started to walk away, then had second thoughts. "Just a word," he said, "I think you should check the plumbing. In my room there was a lot of gurgling throughout the night. Apart from that, my stay here was delightful. Read *Country Life* next month. I'm giving you a favorable review." Then he closed the door behind him and walked to his car.

I nearly fell off my chair. *Fantastic*, I thought. Mr. Bell would be so pleased. Damn plumbing. *Well, it is an old castle, even though all the plumbing is new*, I thought as I put in a call to the plumber.

With my workday behind me, and a feeling of contentment at a successful opening and review, I got ready for my usual Sunday-night call from Dennis. He was eight hours behind me, so it was about lunchtime in California. Tonight, I had put Joanne and Ross to bed early so we could chat alone, although often I let the children speak with him. "So how is it all going, my darling? You sound a little sad," I said.

"The paperwork for the visas is taking longer than it should," he said. "I fired the attorney this week. He was not the right person for our case. He generally works with musicians and such. Besides, he costs a fortune. He's this flamboyant Beverly Hills attorney who really doesn't work for the likes of us who are not in the entertainment world. Anyway, it's like starting all over again. John found us another attorney, who I met with on Friday. So, fingers crossed this one works out and we can get to the next level."

While we were talking about paperwork, I brought up an important date. "I have a court date for the custody hearing at the beginning of April." I heard him sigh. "Oh, Peeps, there's no way my papers will be ready. I won't be there, so that means you'll be alone. What can I do?" I heard the frustration in his voice.

"I'd love for you to be here for moral support, but I understand the bad timing. Mum will be with me, so I won't be alone. I can get through this, although I'm not looking forward to it. I can do this,"

I said, thinking back to yesterday morning when I said the same thing to Fernando and Sharon. And that turned out OK. But this was a lot more complicated, it seemed, than opening a hotel! For one thing, another issue had come up.

"Dennis, I've been advised on my end that we need to make sure we have a house in place by the time I go to court for the custody hearing," I said.

I heard him let out another sigh. "Absolutely. It wouldn't look good if we didn't have a home as a family, so let's decide right now – do you want to live in the Valley or Malibu?"

Honestly, I had no idea. "What's the difference?" Dennis explained that the San Fernando Valley would be more cost effective but really, really hot. And Malibu was closer to Dennis's job, but the price difference to rent was quite a lot.

So far, Dennis and I had relied on our instincts to guide us, so we put them to the test once again. "What does your gut tell you, Dennis?"

"I would prefer to live in Malibu. No doubt we can get over the expense."

"Then let's live in Malibu," I said. "We'll find the money. Decision made."

Our life seemed to be filled with making quick decisions as there was never enough time to ponder over whether something was right or wrong. We made our choice together, then moved in that direction. *I sort of like that!* I thought to myself as I got ready for bed. Hopefully, Dennis would find us somewhere to live in Malibu fast as the court date was just around the corner and we needed that detail in place. So much depended on the outcome of this case as to whether we could go to America.

I woke up on court day feeling I hadn't slept a wink, but I didn't dwell on being tired. I needed to be on top of my game. Joanne and Ross had stayed at Angela's, so the apartment was very tranquil as

I got myself ready over my thoughts and a cup of tea.

At the courthouse, I waited in the common area with our solicitor and my mother. I was wearing my new black suit with a pleated skirt and a button tailored blazer, which I accented with a long-sleeved collared white blouse. I felt I looked professional, and I was feeling good about myself. From what my solicitor had told me, I would need all the confidence I had to get me through this ordeal. Dennis had called to lend his support and remind me to be myself. I had done nothing wrong. Whatever the outcome, we would move forward. I was as ready as I could be.

At some point I had learned that David and Sue had got married in February. Of course. I was sure this was so the judge would see them in a better light. Now that Dennis and I were married, they didn't want to appear to be simply living together. I found that an interesting fact and, again, important to know rather than be surprised by it on the stand.

I had a brief meeting with our Queen's Counsel, or QC, before the hearing. I was feeling a bit scared, but then he turned around and hadn't put his wig on yet. *Ha*, I thought, *we are all human, just going through our days as best we can.* Wigs, robes, outward appearances, all are things that don't matter. What matters is who we are, and I knew that Dennis and I had the children's best interests at heart and would win, no matter which way it went. As I chatted with the QC, I was heartened by his cheerful disposition and air of confidence.

It was soon time for me to take the stand and my oath. I took a deep breath and turned, looking directly in the courtroom. It was not an easy process. The questions were harsh, and I was quickly having to defend myself and my actions from the time we first separated.

David's team painted a picture of me being unstable and giving up the security of a home for the children. They painted my jobs in restaurants and hotels as being nothing but a flimsy interlude, with no future as a real career.

It seemed I was on the stand forever as they kept pounding me with questions of why I did this or that. They continued to say the children were subject to irrational behavior on my part with really no evidence to back that up. They said I was irresponsible, impulsive, and never had the children's best interests at heart.

It was rough going but I had been told simply to answer openly and honestly and not let them get to me. Over lunch with my mum, I had second thoughts. I could barely eat. "I'm not sure how this will turn out."

She nodded her head. "They certainly weren't kind about you, but I think you defended yourself very well and hopefully the judge can see through the lies."

I listened quietly as she continued. "I think the problem is – not that it is a problem from my point of view, but you never know what some people think – you have this drive for better things in life, Pauline. You see opportunity, but not in the way that you would do anything to jeopardize the happiness of Joanne and Ross."

I agreed with that. And I knew it can be hard to get people to understand and see what is in your heart of hearts. I would just have to do my best to tell the judge.

And so right there at the lunch table, I put it all in perspective so I could convey my life and decisions to someone who had never met me. Everything was on the line. I wanted to be with my children, and with Dennis. I wanted us all to be happy. I had focus and drive now, and I was ready to be more.

I met my husband David at eighteen, married at twenty-one, had children at twenty-three and twenty-four, and divorced at twenty-six. There had never been time to think about what I was doing or where my life was going. When I did have the time, the first thing I did was carve a life for myself and the children doing what I love – working in hospitality.

Maybe Blostin's fell in my lap, but I worked hard, learned every aspect of the business, and was able to parlay that into a job at the castle that took us another step along the way to a better life. Now I was faced with yet another opportunity, another step. And it wasn't like planes didn't go back and forth between England and America. I certainly didn't want to take the children away from their father. He was a good dad. In my mind, I was bringing them closer to a better future, and myself too.

By now, my mum was holding my hand and nodding. "Yes, and look at them now. Joanne and Ross are just fine and that is because you created security for them and gave them the love they need. Let's hope the judge sees that."

David and I had not spoken a word to each other from the first moment we walked into the courthouse. We stayed as far apart as we could through this whole process. After I took the stand and told my side of the story, the cross-examination was over. Nothing more needed to be said. Now it was time for the judge's verdict.

I wanted to vomit as I waited to hear what the judge had to say. It was all a blur until I heard the words. "Even if Mrs. Parry did decide California was not agreeable to the family and decided to take another direction in their life journey, the children would not be affected by the disruption and would take it in their stride. I therefore grant Mrs. Parry sole custody of the children."

With that, I heard the hammer go down and the words "court dismissed."

I sank in my chair in disbelief at what I'd just heard. My mother came over to me and put her arms around me. I glanced over at David and Sue, whose looks were thunderous! They didn't say a word and walked out of the courtroom. Later, of course, we were able to speak in friendly terms, and worked out a nice arrangement that would ensure the children and their father remained close. But for now, I couldn't wait to get home and tell Dennis the news.

"Are you sitting down?" I said when I got him on the phone. I took a pause. "We have sole custody!"

There was silence. I think I could hear the tension being released from his body as I waited for him to speak. "I'm speechless, Peeps. I'm so excited I could burst."

"Me too!" I said, laughing and crying. All we needed to do now was secure the visas.

It was about another month before Dennis could get his papers to leave the country and permits to work in America, which was the start of the process of getting a green card. It seems like we had all these uncertainties constantly going on, but we were always confident that it would work out.

So there we were, with a new home, a clear direction for the children, and our visas for America in hand. After five months of not knowing what the future would hold for us, we were on the last leg. I wasn't sure how to feel and if those butterflies in my stomach were joy or fear. *Anything could still happen*, I thought. We were still living a continent apart and communicating mostly through letters and a weekly phone call. But I was happy with what I had.

And we had one more round of frantic plane flights, packing, and moving. There was a lot to keep my mind busy. Dennis would be back in June to get all the details in place and say our goodbyes to our family and loved ones in England.

I couldn't believe we were actually at this point. In one of our Sunday calls, when he told me he had our tickets, I admitted, "I think I'm feeling a bit emotional and want to cry."

He agreed. "I know what you mean. I feel the same way. It's a bit surreal. But it's happening. I can assure you of that," he said, with a great gush of certainty. *Love that*, I thought.

"OK then, I'll see you in a couple of weeks. I can't believe I am finally saying that," I chuckled. "Till then, sending you kisses and so much more, bye, bye, bye…" I trailed off, not wanting to put the phone down. As I did, I just stared at the phone, not sure how to feel. The end of these phone calls was always hard. *But not for much longer*, I thought as I turned off the light and got ready for another day.

Duck Confit with Red Currant Sauce Served with Lentils and Crispy Pancetta

Critic's choice! This was the meal the very first food and travel writer I have ever met had at the castle. He loved it and his stay there and gave us a good write-up. I guarantee you'll have a good write-up from whomever you make this dish for too!

Serves 4

Duck Confit

4 duck legs	*2 dried bay leaves, crumbled*
½ cup coarse sea salt	*4 teaspoons brandy*
2 ounces cracked black pepper	*25 ounces duck fat*
1 head of garlic, separated into cloves	*You will also need:*
8 sprigs fresh thyme	*plastic wrap*

Rub the duck legs with the salt, black pepper, 2 crushed garlic cloves, half the thyme, and the bay leaves. Pack tightly into a dish, skin side down, then add the brandy. Cover with plastic wrap and let marinate in the refrigerator for 24 hours.

Preheat the oven to 300°F.

Scrape the marinade off the duck legs. Heat the duck fat in a heavy ovenproof dish, then add the duck and the remaining garlic cloves and thyme. The duck legs should be completely submerged in the melted fat. Cook, covered, in the oven for 3 hours. Remove from the oven and let cool, uncovered.

Preheat the oven to 350°F.

Place the duck on a sheet pan and cook for about 30 minutes, until the skin is crispy brown.

Pancetta Lentils

5 ounces shaved pancetta

2 carrots, peeled and finely diced

2 onions, peeled and chopped

10 ounces cooked green lentils

4 quarts of chicken stock

1 tablespoon chopped parsley

Meanwhile, prepare the lentils. In a medium saucepan, sear the shaved pancetta until lightly browned. Add the carrots and onions and cook for about 10 minutes, until softened. Add the lentils and chicken stock. Bring to a boil, then reduce to a simmer for 10 minutes. Stir in the chopped parsley.

Red Currant Sauce

1 cup good red wine

1 tablespoon red currant jelly

1 teaspoon balsamic vinegar

2 cups chicken stock

1 knob of butter

Place the red wine, red currant jelly, and balsamic vinegar in a small saucepan and reduce on medium-low heat until it starts to get sticky and dark. Add the chicken stock and reduce by three-fourths. Remove from the heat and whisk in the knob of butter.

Serve the duck with the pancetta lentils and drizzle with the red currant sauce.

Warm Crab Cake Layered with Phyllo Pastry Feuilletée

This is also based on a dish that the food and travel writer enjoyed at Thornbury. I've made it now for guests many times and it always gets rave reviews!

Serves 4

Phyllo Layers

1 packet store-bought phyllo sheets   *½ cup melted unsalted butter*

Preheat the oven to 350°F.

Place one sheet of phyllo pastry on a clean dry surface and brush with melted butter. Place another sheet of phyllo on top and again brush with melted butter. Repeat until you have 4 sheets of pastry together. Cut out twelve 2 × 4-inch rectangles. Place on a sheet tray and bake for 10 minutes, until golden brown.

Crab Salad

1 pound Dungeness crab meat, flaked
4 teaspoons finely sliced fresh chives
1 teaspoon minced fresh tarragon leaves
⅓ cup mayonnaise
3 tablespoons sour cream
1 teaspoon freshly squeezed lemon juice
½ teaspoon Dijon mustard
kosher salt and freshly ground pepper
watercress and chives, for garnish

In a medium bowl, lightly toss the flaked crabmeat, chives, and tarragon together.

In a small bowl, stir together the mayonnaise, sour cream, lemon juice, and mustard. Add the dressing to the crabmeat mixture and stir until just coated. Season to taste with salt and pepper.

To assemble

For each serving, place one sheet of cooked phyllo as the foundation. Add crabmeat salad to cover. Place another phyllo sheet on top of the crabmeat and add another layer of crabmeat salad. Top with another phyllo sheet.

Garnish with watercress and chives. If desired, drizzle with a lemon beurre blanc (see John Dory Fillet, page 189) for extra richness.

CHAPTER EIGHTEEN
California Here We Come

In fairy tales, the princess usually moves into the castle to begin living happily ever after with her true love. Instead, I was leaving the castle and would be moving to places unknown, somewhere in California. At least I got it right when it came to the part about living happily ever after with my true love.

I had to laugh and yet, as I prepared to leave my castle forever, I felt a twinge of sorrow. It had been a very special place for me, even with all the difficulties I had faced working there, the nights that I felt alone with Dennis gone, and the times I worried about the children and custody. But there were many great memories too. It was where I had learned how to open a hotel, learned the ins and outs of a new level of culinary discovery, and of course, was able to live with the children in such amazing surroundings.

I smiled and gave a heavy sigh as I left the key on the windowsill for the next person to enjoy this lovely little gatehouse. I noticed that the grapevines had just come in bloom as I walked for the last time down the flagstone stairs and across the courtyard to the office to say goodbye to Mr. Bell.

As usual he was sitting at his desk, doing some paperwork.

He got up when he saw me. He had just finished writing a letter. "Pauline," he said sweetly, "you'll be missed. I'm the first to admit that we had a tricky start. I had a moment when I wondered if you'd make it here, but by gosh if you didn't prove me wrong!" I blushed as he handed me the letter, which I then realized was a letter of reference. I hadn't asked for it, but it was so like him to do that.

"Oh, Mr. Bell, that's so kind. Thank you for everything. This has certainly been some journey. I'll remember it for the rest of my life," I said, feeling a little sense of loss. We shook hands and he assured me that I was always welcome back. Of course, I hoped it would never come to that, but it was touching to hear him say it.

As I walked out, it was like walking through memories. I could see Joanne and Ross on stools at the kitchen counter eating breakfast, the postman who always brought me letters from Dennis, all my friends there who had worked long hours with me to get the hotel ready, and of course the meals and wine that I'd enjoyed with Mr. Bell. I smiled as I left through the kitchen door, closing it tightly behind me.

There wasn't much more to do. I had sold or given away all our furniture and even a lot of Joanne and Ross's toys. We had arranged to put the MG in storage. Dennis had sold his car but not his house. Rich was still living there, so we would deal with that later. With really nothing left but a few suitcases, the children and I had moved in for a very short time with my mum and dad. Dennis had been gone for five months while I closed the "castle" and got us ready to go.

The night before Dennis was due to come back from America one last time, I was in my parents' kitchen late. I must have been deep in thought with my glass of wine. I didn't hear my mum come in until she said, "What are you thinking about, Pauline?"

"Oh, I was just thinking that I hope we've done the right thing. Sometimes I have doubts. I'm feeling a little scared."

As usual, she knew the right thing to say. "That's natural. You're about to go on an enormous adventure. Just be sure you and Dennis enjoy the ride. You'll have difficulties and challenges but I have no doubt you will take them in your stride," she said as she hugged me tight.

The next day, once again, I drove to Heathrow to pick up Dennis. This would be the last time. The next time we'd all be leaving together as a family. These last months had been tough, with so much to do and being so far apart. But I was grateful for the love letters I received every day from him. They were sometimes so vivid that I felt like I was in his arms. I believe it was the letters that kept a bond between us, giving us the strength to deal with all the ups and downs of our lives apart.

And then there he was, walking toward me looking handsome, tall and tanned, my husband. I felt a rush of warmth to my cheeks. He swept me in his arms, and as always, we didn't say a word to each other. We just kissed.

Once in the car, I said, "I'll let you know how to get to the Athenaeum Hotel."

He looked at me with surprise. "That's right!" I cried out. "We have a night out in London!" I said with a huge giggle.

"Alright, take me there, Mrs. Parry," he said, smiling while putting his foot on the accelerator.

This was our third time at the hotel. The first was my thirtieth birthday. The second was before he left for America the first time. And this was the third. "I love this tradition," Dennis said as we were walking to The Ritz for dinner.

We sat in a window seat at the restaurant. Wherever we go, I always ask for the corner table or a window seat. I hate sitting in the middle of the room, it always makes me feel insecure. When I said this to Dennis the first time, he smiled and said, "You?! Insecure? I have a hard time believing that."

A glass of Krug champagne went perfectly with our Salmon Tartare served with a soft-boiled egg and toast points. As we were enjoying it, Dennis noted a table of six people opposite us. "Look, they're American."

"Oh, how do you know?"

"Simple, they aren't wearing any socks." I looked and indeed they weren't. I would never have noticed. "That seems to be the thing in the States now."

I laughed heartily. "I know you'd never be that man!" Dennis was a traditional man to the tips of his toes, literally.

Dinner was leisurely. We ordered an Echezeaux wine, one of the first wines we'd shared together. It went perfectly with the beef fillet topped with a truffle mushroom butter. We talked and talked about the future and about what had happened these last five months. Everything we talked about was in our letters, which I loved reading, but to hear some of the same stories in person was quite refreshing. *It's as if the person who wrote the letters is now reading them to me,* I mused.

We finished our wine with an array of artisan English cheeses followed by a caramelized peach crêpe. A Muscat de Beaumes de Venise with dessert reminded me of our meals at the castle. It was the perfect ending to twenty-four hours back together.

"They say all good things come to an end," I said as we were now driving down the M4 home to Mum and Dad's. "Joanne and Ross are excited to see you," I added, and that made Dennis smile. "I'm also looking forward to having a pint with your dad in the pub," he said. The one thing he couldn't get in America. "We can accommodate that request," I smiled back.

That was one of the last quiet times together. The next eight days were a flurry of activity as we wrapped up all the details and said our goodbyes.

Everyone wished us well and they were excited for us, but it was a tremendously emotional time that felt hard to bear sometimes. One of the hardest moments was the dreadful parting of the children and their father. It was heartbreaking. I never wanted to go through that again and I knew Joanne, Ross, and David didn't. My only consolation was that it wasn't forever. We had worked it out so they would go back to England to see David every summer for six to eight weeks and sometimes they went for trips in-between. It turned out to be very amicable, which was so important to me for the children and David.

Saying goodbye to Mum, even though we'd fly back and forth, was one of those moments that hurt. "I'll write you a letter every week, Mum. I promise. And when we get settled, we'll send you a ticket to come over so you can see for yourself what our life is like." After a huge hug, we had to make our final goodbyes or risk missing our flight. "We'll call when we get in, whatever time that is," I said. We watched her from the rear window waving to us until she was out of sight.

For the first half hour of the two-hour drive to the airport, we were all alone with our thoughts. Dad was driving and the car was quiet. I'm not sure Joanne and Ross completely grasped the magnitude of the move, which made it easier on Dennis and myself.

We had two suitcases each. Dad helped us load them on the cart outside the airport. "Dad," – I was holding back tears – "please say goodbye here. I don't think I can take any more!" He was lost for words for the very first time, as he always had something to say – either words of wisdom or the love he wanted to share. But today, after he gave us all a kiss and a hug, he was silent, tears rolling down his face as he got in the car. He blew us one more kiss before driving off. My heart was heavy as I watched him leave.

"I hope it's not this emotional every time we leave," I said to Dennis as we finally settled on the plane. "I don't know if I can take it."

Of course, it was all lost on Joanne and Ross. They had never flown before and so were fascinated and excited about the experience. As the pilot was walking down the aisle, he stopped to chat with us and the children. Once he learned this was their first time on a plane, he asked, "Would you like to come up to the flight deck and see how we fly the airplane?" They were up in a flash and ran behind him to the cockpit. Dennis went with them.

I couldn't help but think that this was a good sign – an opportunity they might never have had, had we not been starting a new life in a new country.

Dennis had arranged for his friend Craig to pick us up. As our new little family of four waited on the curb, a little worse for wear from the busy week we had just had and the long flight, a huge black limousine pulled up in front of us. I had never seen a car this big. And just then Craig got out of the back of the car, and with a big smile asked, "Can I give you a lift?" The children were beside themselves and jumped in.

There was champagne on ice, which Craig poured as we left the airport. "I'd like to make a toast," he said. I was delighted by the gesture, never one to turn down a glass of champagne or a toast! "May your new life bring you an abundance of joy and happiness. Cheers to a great future!" With that, he opened the roof so the children could stand up and pop their heads out, letting the wind blow through their hair. They were screaming with delight.

I smiled as I watched them. What a wonderful experience and adventure this was going to be, everything so new and different. Who knew what lay ahead but I had no doubt in my mind, whatever it was, it was going to be fabulous!

We stopped at the Market Basket supermarket to get food. Dennis had already stocked the house with non-disposable essentials, but we needed food for dinner. We were all giddy – even Joanne and Ross seemed excited at what we saw in the market, which was huge compared to English stores. We walked out with a ton of brown bags, the bags themselves a novelty for us all.

We drove through Malibu along the coast, passing beautiful sights of the ocean and beaches before turning off on Corral Canyon. We took the winding mountain roads for about two miles. We were all so excited about where we were going and seeing our new home.

Dennis said as we turned off onto Cool Glen, "This is the final turn, look ahead." At the top of a driveway we could see an A-frame cabin, with an orange car parked under a carport.

We all jumped out of the car as we were bursting with anticipation to see where we would be living. Dennis had sent me photos and although this was not a Thornbury Castle, it was *our* castle, and I was grinning from ear to ear.

It was a small cabin that simply had one large room with a kitchen area, a place for a dining table and chairs and a large lounge with a stone fireplace, and all we had in the room was one sofa.

There were two bedrooms with a bathroom between. Dennis had built the beds. The rooms were only big enough to fit one double bed for us and bunk beds for Joanne and Ross. "I'm the top," Joanne said as she was climbing up the ladder, not giving Ross a chance to choose. Dennis had bought mattresses and bedding and had made the beds ready for our arrival.

Dennis said to Joanne and Ross, "Close your eyes, we have a surprise for you, hold my hand," as he guided them outside. "Now you can open your eyes!" What followed were screams of delight, followed with pleas of "Can we get in?" The house had a swimming pool.

They could not contain themselves with excitement. "You don't need swimsuits. Just take off your clothes," I said. And with that they dropped their clothes to the ground and jumped in with a massive splash.

That night we ate, we drank champagne, the children swam, Craig hung out with us until his driver needed to be off the clock. "Thanks, Craig. You've made our arrival in America very special and we're so grateful you could do this for us," I said as he made his exit to go home.

"It was my pleasure. This was priceless, seeing you and the children react to everything. Dennis, see you at work Monday?"

"I'll be there!" Dennis smiled.

By now, Joanne and Ross had fallen asleep on the sofa with towels wrapped around them. The jet lag was getting the better of them – after all, it would have been six o'clock in the morning if they were in England.

We carried them both into their beds. The evening was so warm, they didn't need pajamas. We gave them a kiss. They were half asleep, turning over to get in a comfortable position, and were in a blissfully deep sleep before we left the room.

It already felt like home. It was dark outside and the light in the room was the perfect glow. Our suitcases were open, clothes were everywhere. *Who cares? We have tomorrow to sort all that out.*

My thoughts flashed back to how we got here and, more to the point, how Dennis came into my life. Who knew that a chance dinner at Blostin's would not only lead me to him but would ignite my passion for food and wine – something I had no idea about a couple of years ago? And that both Dennis and food would become a lifelong passion of mine?

Dennis refreshed our champagne glasses. We curled up together on the sofa. I let out a soft sigh. My culinary love story had had a happy ending. From my beginnings as a young mother in a suburban neighborhood to a flat above a restaurant, to an apartment on castle grounds and, now, to a home in Malibu, I felt ready for a new kitchen, one that was truly my own.

"I can't believe we are here. What do we do now?" I said, laughing.

"Don't worry about that tonight – we have our whole life ahead of us, we'll work it all out tomorrow," he said, giving me a kiss that lasted way into the night.

"Tomorrow it is," I said.

Salmon Tartare with a Quail Egg

An elegant beginning that was part of a beautiful ending for me as Dennis and I prepared to leave England. The fresh salmon and smoked salmon fillet go beautifully with a soft-boiled quail egg.

Serves 6

1 pound skinless fresh salmon fillet
½ pound smoked salmon
⅓ cup freshly squeezed lime juice
⅓ cup minced shallots
2 tablespoons extra virgin olive oil
¼ cup minced fresh dill
3 tablespoons drained capers
2 tablespoons Dijon mustard
1 tablespoon whole grain mustard
2 tablespoons sea salt flakes

1 teaspoon coarsely ground black
  pepper
6 quail eggs
¼ cup minced fresh parsley
1 loaf of sliced bread of choice, toasted
  for serving

You will also need:
plastic wrap

Cut the fresh and smoked salmon into ¼-inch dice. Place the salmon in a mixing bowl and add the lime juice, shallots, olive oil, dill, capers, Dijon and whole grain mustards, salt and pepper. Mix well, cover with plastic wrap, and refrigerate for a few hours for the salmon to marinate.

In a small saucepan, bring an inch of water to a boil and add the quail eggs. Cook for 2½ minutes. Remove and immediately place in cold water to cool. Once cold, peel the eggs.

When ready to serve, toast the bread and cut into triangles.

Divide the tartare between six plates. Cut each egg in half and place on top. Sprinkle with chopped parsley and serve with the toast points.

Filet Mignon with Porcini Mushroom Truffle Butter

If you are a steak lover, there is nothing better than filet mignon, especially when it is topped with a wild mushroom compound butter with black truffles!

Serves 6

Steaks

6 filet mignon steaks, 5–6 ounces each
kosher salt and freshly ground pepper
1 tablespoon butter

1 teaspoon olive oil
2 cloves of garlic, thinly sliced
4 sprigs of fresh thyme

Preheat the oven to 475°F.

Season the steaks generously with kosher salt and freshly ground black pepper – more than you think, as much of it comes off during the cooking process.

Heat a cast-iron skillet on the stove top over high heat. Melt the butter in the olive oil. Add the steaks and cook for about 3 minutes on each side, until browned.

Remove from the heat, add the sliced garlic and thyme sprigs, and cook in the oven until the internal temperature reaches 140°F for medium rare.

Porcini Mushroom Truffle Butter

10 whole porcini mushrooms
½ ounce dried porcini mushrooms
1 cup salted butter, at room temperature

½ ounce whole black truffle, sliced
salt
You will also need:
plastic wrap

Place the whole porcini mushrooms in a small bowl. Add just enough boiling water to cover the mushrooms. Cover and set aside for 5–10 minutes, or until the mushrooms have reconstituted and are soft. Drain the mushrooms and squeeze out the excess water. Thinly slice the mushrooms and set aside.

Finely grind the dried porcini mushrooms in a coffee grinder.

Place the butter in a food processor fitted with a metal blade. Add 2 tablespoons of the porcini powder, half the porcini mushroom slices, and half the black truffle slices. Season to taste with salt. Blend until well mixed and the butter is smooth.

Using a rubber spatula, scrape the butter onto a sheet of plastic wrap. Roll into a log shape. Place the reserved porcini slices on top of the butter and wrap tightly. Twist the ends of the plastic wrap to seal. Refrigerate for 30 minutes or until cold enough to slice.

When ready to serve, remove the porcini butter compound from the refrigerator and slice into ½-inch pats. Remove the steaks from the oven, spoon over the cooking juices, and serve garnished with a pat of porcini butter and the remaining black truffle slices.

Caramelized Peach Crêpe

A sweet ending for us all. A light buttery crêpe served with caramelized peaches with a dollop of mascarpone whipped cream and a fresh mint garnish.

Serves 6

Crêpes

¾ cup all-purpose flour	*1⅓ cups whole milk*
¾ teaspoon salt	*1 ounce butter, melted, plus 1 ounce*
3 large eggs, lightly whisked	*for pan*

Combine the flour and salt in a blender. Blend in the eggs, milk, and melted butter on high speed for 1 minute. Scrape down the sides and blend for a further 30 seconds. If the batter is still lumpy, strain it through a sieve. Cover and let rest at room temperature for at least an hour.

Heat an 8-inch pan or skillet over medium-high heat. Brush with melted butter. Using a ¼ cup measure, scoop out the batter and pour it into the skillet. Pick up the pan and swirl it so the batter covers the base. Cook for about 1 minute until they bubble and brown, then loosen the edges of the crêpe with a spatula. Using a spatula, turn the crêpe over. Cook the other side until lightly golden. Slide it onto a plate and cover with wax paper. Repeat with the remaining batter.

The coulis and topping can be made while the crêpe batter is resting. Refrigerate until you are ready to serve.

Coulis

1 large fresh peach, peeled and chopped *2 teaspoons sugar*
2 tablespoons amaretto

Combine the chopped peach, amaretto, and sugar in a small sauce-pan over medium heat. Cook, stirring, for 10 minutes, until the peach is soft. Remove from the heat and let cool. Pour the mixture into the bowl of a food processor and puree. Pour into a jug and refrigerate until ready to serve.

Topping

2 tablespoons butter

¼ cup brown sugar

1 peach, peeled and sliced

2 ounces heavy cream

2 ounces mascarpone

1 tablespoon amaretto

mint sprigs, for garnish

Melt the butter in a skillet over medium low heat, add the sugar, and lightly poach the peach slices. Let cool.

Lightly whip the cream into soft peaks then gently stir in the mascarpone and amaretto until blended. Refrigerate until ready to serve.

To serve, fold each crêpe into a triangle. Top with the mascarpone whipped cream and poached peach slices. Swirl the coulis over the crêpes and garnish with a mint sprig.

List of Recipes

Starters

Entrees

Entrees continued

Sides

Desserts

———

Drinks

———